Conte

Introduction

Reading comprehension is the cornerstone of a child's academic success. By completing the activities in this book, children will develop and reinforce essential reading comprehension skills. Children will benefit from a wide variety of opportunities to practice engaging with text as active readers who can self-monitor their understanding of what they have read.

Children will focus on the following:

Identifying the Purpose of the Text
- The reader understands, and can tell you, why they read the text.

Understanding the Text
- What is the main idea of the text?
- What are the supporting details?
- Which parts are facts and which parts are opinions?

Analyzing the Text
- How does the reader's background knowledge enhance the text clues to help the reader answer questions about the text or draw conclusions?
- What inferences can be made by using information from the text with what the reader already knows?
- How does the information from the text help the reader make predictions?
- What is the cause and effect between events?

Making Connections
How does the topic or information they are reading remind the reader about what they already know?
- Text-to-self connections: How does this text relate to your own life?
- Text-to-text connections: Have I read something like this before? How is this text similar to something I have read before? How is this text different from something I have read before?
- Text-to-world connections: What does this text remind you of in the real world?

Using Text Features
- How do different text features help the reader?

Text Features

Text features help the reader to understand the text better. Here is a list of text features with a brief explanation of how they help the reader.

Contents	Here the reader will find the title of each section, what page each text starts on within sections, and where to find specific information.
Chapter Title	The chapter title gives the reader an idea of what the text will be about. The chapter title is often followed by subheadings within the text.
Title and Subheading	The title or topic is found at the top of the page. The subheading is right above a paragraph. There may be more than one subheading in a text.
Map	Maps help the reader understand where something is happening. It is a visual representation of a location.
Diagram and Illustration	Diagrams and illustrations give the reader additional visual information about the text.
Label	A label tells the reader the title of a map, diagram, or illustration. Labels also draw attention to specific elements within a visual.
Caption	Captions are words that are placed underneath the visuals. Captions give the reader more information about the map, diagram, or illustration.
Fact Box	A fact box tells the reader extra information about the topic.
Table	A table presents text information in columns and rows in a concise and often comparative way.
Bold and Italic text	**Bold** and *italic* text are used to emphasize a word or words, and signify that this is important vocabulary.

How to Be a Good Babysitter

Aaron, age 6

- no allergies
- likes a banana before going to bed
- bedtime is 8
- leave night light on
- Mrs. Crawford 555-795-8512
- Mrs. Singh (neighbour) 555-754-9923

Have you ever babysat for a younger brother or sister? Have family, friends, or neighbours asked you to babysit? Would you like to earn some money by babysitting?

Babysitting is often a first job for young people like you. But babysitting is more than just a job. It is a great responsibility. When you babysit, you are responsible for another person. It is your job to keep that person safe, healthy, and happy. That is quite a lot to ask. So how can you make sure that you can do the job well? Here are some very important tips to follow to help.

1. **Take a babysitting course.** Courses are often offered through schools, hospitals, or community organizations. Most courses focus on child safety and first aid.
2. **Learn about the child you will be babysitting before you do the job.** This will mean a visit with the parents or adult you will be working for. Find out as much as you can about the child. Allergies and fears are very important things to know, as well as favourite foods and games. Write down what you learn.
3. **Ask about household rules.** What time does the child go to bed? Can the child watch television? For how long? Which shows? What snacks can the child have? Remember that you are taking the place of the parents and need to follow their rules. You are responsible for the house too. Make sure you keep everything clean and tidy.
4. **Make sure you have a written contact list.** You should know how to contact the parents. As a backup, it is good to get the phone number of another adult that you could call in case you cannot contact the parents. Also have emergency numbers written down.
5. **Plan what you are going to do with the child.** Plan games that the child might like to play. Think about books you can read together. Doing something is always better than sitting in front of a Television or a video game.
6. **Stay focussed on the job.** Your main responsibility is to the child, so do not phone or text friends when you should be watching the child.
7. **Have fun.** Say positive things, smile, and laugh. The more fun you have with the child, the happier the child will be with you. Most children will be anxious when their parents leave, so it is important to make babysitting a positive experience for both of you.

If you do not feel ready to babysit but would like to in the future, think about being a helper. A helper is someone who looks after children while the parents are home. This will give you experience but with less responsibility. You can also talk to others who babysit. Find out what they do that works well. Read about babysitting on the Internet or in books. The more you know, the more prepared you will be to try babysitting—and to do a great job.

"How to Be a Good Babysitter"—Think About It

1. What does the author suggest you do if you are not ready to try babysitting yet?

He says if you want to baby sit then take the course it would be helpful about babysitting and it was

2. Why is it important to know things such as a child's fears or allergies?

It is inportant to know all these things because it is your responsapity to take of him. for example he is scared of bed time you know that and help him out.

3. This text includes a numbered list. How is this list different from one you might find in a text that is telling you how to make something?

It is telling to do the things in order. It is different because it is informative and there is alot of info unlike a process

4. What is the author's point of view in this text? How does the author support this point of view?

He proves his point by putting in articals and has a lot of info.

5. What does the author mean by the sentence "That is quite a lot to ask"? Use specific details from the text to support your answer.

It means that is alot of work but in the end you should enjoy and have fun.

6. Do you think this text is fact or opinion? How do you know? Explain your ideas fully.

I think that some of is opinion and other is fact. The opinon how it done and the process. But the fact is how it's done and how to do it.

Build Up That Body

We all know that being physically fit is a good thing. Being fit helps you keep your body at a healthy weight, helps prevent some diseases, makes you feel better mentally, gives you more energy, and helps you sleep better. Physical fitness has different parts or components. Four of these are muscle strength, muscle endurance, flexibility, and cardiovascular fitness.

Muscle Strength

Muscle strength is the amount of force a muscle can produce or exert. Some types of exercise can make your muscles stronger. When your muscles are stronger, you can do everyday things more easily. And when you strengthen your muscles, you are strengthening your bones as well. When your muscles push and pull against your bones, this makes your bones stronger. Some activities and exercises that will build stronger muscles and bones are doing push-ups, playing tug-of-war, climbing stairs, running, yoga, and bike riding.

Muscle Endurance

Muscle endurance is different from muscle strength. Muscle endurance is how many times or for how long a muscle can exert a force. Muscle endurance is very important if you play a sport or game that lasts for a long time. Sports such as football, hockey, tennis, and cross-country running will help improve muscle endurance. Upper body exercises such as push-ups and chin-ups will help improve endurance and strength too.

Flexibility

Flexibility is how far your muscles can stretch. When you are flexible, you can move your arms and legs freely without feeling tightness or pain. You can bend and stretch easily. Exercise and activities you can do for good flexibility include gymnastics, ballet, and martial arts. Or you can do simple stretches such as touching your toes and bending your body from side to side.

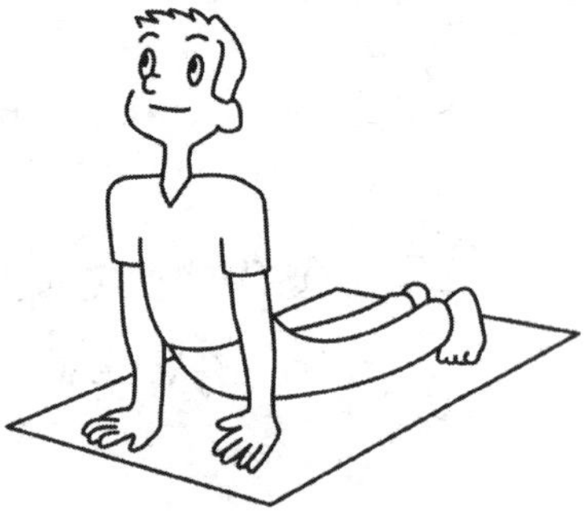

Cardiovascular Fitness

Your heart pumps blood around your body through blood vessels. Your blood carries oxygen to all parts of your body. Cardiovascular fitness is a measure of how well your heart pumps blood to deliver oxygen. When you do activities or an exercise that make your heart pump faster, it gets better at doing its job. Anything that makes your heart beat faster and gets you breathing faster will help your heart improve. So go ahead and swim, play basketball, run, inline skate, jump rope, or cross-country ski. Your heart will thank you.

"Build Up That Body"—Think About It

1. How do your muscles help your bones? Use evidence from the text to support your answer.

They push and pull on your bones. Which mak your bones and mucels stroger

2. How do cardiovascular activities affect your heart? Write the sentence in the text that helped you find this answer.

your heart pumps blood thru vessel and that fitness makes it faster and bett en

3. How can flexibility help your body do everyday things? What do you think might happen if you were not very flexible?

It can help with everything exersice actives etc.

4. What conclusions can you make about different types of activities and their connection to different components of physical fitness? Support your ideas with examples from the text.

exercis should be a part of your every day scedaule. It should be because it help your body.

5. Cardio refers to the heart. Vascular refers to blood vessels. Which component of physical fitness uses these terms and why?

6. What is the main idea of the introductory paragraph? How does the author expand on this idea?

Do It Safely

You know how important physical activity is for your body. When you get your body moving, you are keeping your body healthy now and for the future. You can play a team sport such as hockey or baseball. You can do classes in yoga or aerobics. You can train to take part in a run. You can play with your friends at the park or ride your bikes together.

You should do different activities so all parts of your body get a workout. You should exercise regularly. But the most important thing is to enjoy what you do. If you like something, you will do it more often.

Keeping Safe

No matter what you do, it is important to do it safely. Here are some tips to help you keep safe.

- Choose the proper equipment. Wear the proper helmet for your activity. A bicycle helmet is different from a helmet you would wear to play hockey. Protect your eyes. Wear the proper goggles or face guards for the activity. If you wear glasses, get a prescription pair of goggles. Do not wear your regular glasses to play a sport.

  Wear a mouth guard to protect your mouth and teeth for sports such as football. Wear pads to protect parts of your body for activities such as skateboarding. Wear the proper footwear for the activity. And make sure your footwear is in good shape. Worn-out shoes can be dangerous. Know how to use your equipment properly.

- Warm up for any activity or exercise. If you are riding your bike, start off slowly. Give your muscles a chance to move before working them too hard. Before playing a sport, do some easy jogging or walking. Then do some stretches to warm up your muscles.

- Give your body time to heal if you hurt yourself. And if you do get an injury, stop what you are doing right away. Do not exercise if you are sick. Wait until you are feeling better.

- Follow the rules of the game you are playing. Rules not only keep a game fair, but they protect the people playing. And follow the rules of the road if you are inline skating or riding your bike.

Now get out there and have fun!

"Do It Safely"—Think About It

1. The author describes three things to do to get the most out of physical activity. What are these?

Choose the right equpement. warm up. Give your body sometime.

2. Why should you warm up before doing an activity? Do you think you would need to warm up before going for an easy walk? Why or why not?

You should warm up because to give your mucels to move them.

3. Why should you stop as soon as you get an injury? What might happen if you did not stop?

You should stop because you chould get a more severe injury.

4. Write a summary of the "tips to help keep you safe."

Choose the right stuff allways wear a helmet. Wear the proper protcolon for your activity/sport. Allways warm up do something light before you do something heavy. take time off when injured

5. What is the relationship between equipment and safety during physical activity? Use specific details from the text to support your answer.

It helps you protect yourself and also they all are very widely used and they all help your body.

Treating Minor Injuries

Minor injuries can happen anytime—when you are playing a sport or game, when you are exercising, or when you are just fooling around with friends. It is important to know how to treat minor injuries so they get better faster. It is also very important to know when you should see a doctor.

Strains and Sprains

A **strain** is when a muscle has stretched too far and tears a little. A **sprain** is an injury to the ligaments that hold a muscle to a bone. Ligaments can stretch and tear, just like a muscle. If you think you have a strain or a sprain, stop your activity immediately so there is no pressure or weight on the injured part. To treat minor strains or sprains, follow the PRICE rule:

- **P**rotect the injured part from further injury.
- **R**est the injured part.
- **I**ce or cold compresses should be applied several times a day to reduce swelling.
- **C**ompress the area with a splint or elastic bandage to prevent swelling. Do not make the bandage too tight, though.
- **E**levate the injured part so that it is above your heart.

Apply ice to reduce swelling

When to see a doctor: You should see a doctor if the pain is very bad, you cannot move or put weight on the injured part, the injured area feels numb, you heard a popping sound when the injury occurred, or the injured part is oddly bent. Sometimes a bad sprain can really be a bone fracture so it is better to be safe than sorry.

Scrapes and Cuts

If you are bleeding, apply pressure to the cut or scrape for 5 to 10 minutes. The bleeding should stop by then. Wash the wound with plain water. Look carefully to see if there is anything in the wound. Put on an antiseptic ointment and cover with a bandage that will keep out air and water.

When to see a doctor: You should see a doctor if the wound does not stop bleeding after applying pressure; the cut has ragged edges or is very long or deep; or the wound begins to look red or infected, is draining pus, or becomes painful to touch.

Blisters

We usually do not think of blisters as an injury, but they are. Blisters can be very painful and stop you from doing many activities until they heal. If you get a blister, wash the area with soap and warm water. Apply a cold pack to reduce swelling. Keep the area around the blister clean and dry. Do not burst the blister. If the blister does break, put a bandage over it to keep the area clean.

When to see a doctor: Look for signs of infection. The blister might get hot, swell, become red, or become painful. There might be red streaks on the skin coming from the blister area. There might be pus or other fluid coming from the blister. You might get a fever. If any of these things happen, see a doctor right away.

"Treating Minor Injuries"—Think About It

1. What is the difference between a strain and a sprain? Which might be more serious? Use examples from the text to support your answer.

A strain is when a muscle has stretched to far. A sprain is an injury to the ligament.

2. What do you think might happen if you wound a bandage too tightly around a strain or sprain?

because it would put a lot or weight and that is relly bad.

3. What is the central or main idea of this text?

The main idea is how to treat a minor injury and how it occurs.

4. PRICE is an acronym. The letters in an acronym are each the first letter of a word. The acronym is pronounced as a word. What words does PRICE stand for? How do you know?

It stands for the afects and how your going to deal with it. I know becuse it fits in the sentce and that what it most likely means.

5. The author uses the phrase "it is better to be safe than sorry." What does this mean? How does this phrase fit with the topic of the text?

It means that safer to be safe and have to take extra percautions and sorry means that you were to risky and you could make it worse

6. Following the introductory paragraph, three injuries are described. How are the descriptions the same? How could the author have presented this information in a different way using a graphic organizer?

Maybe by combing scrapes and cuts with straies and sprains

Blog or News?

Is it a blog or is it news? Do you know the difference between a blog and a news report or article? You can find both on many websites, and sometimes they will be about the same subject. Read the following two items that were posted on a book publisher's website:

> *On April 23, the new book by Ana Grimley arrived for sale in bookstores across the country. Her new book is called* The Far Away Country, *a sequel to her first book,* Closer to Home. *The two books are the first in a planned series of four, which together will complete the journey of the book's hero, Justine Waverley. Justine was introduced in* Closer to Home. *In this book, the readers learned about this extraordinary young woman and the problems faced by her family and the town she lived in. In* The Far Away Country, *Justine leaves to find a solution and travels to a place full of danger, but also full of hope.* The Far Away Country *is written for middle readers, ages 9 to 12. This 137-page softcover book has a suggested price of $11.99.*

> *The long-awaited sequel to* Closer to Home *has finally arrived. And it was worth the wait.* The Far Away Country *is even better than the first book. It will keep you glued to the pages, long past the time when you should be asleep. The author, Ana Grimley, has invented a new world so amazing and dazzling, it comes alive in your mind. And Justine once again proves she is no ordinary young woman. This book was written for 9- to 12-year-olds but, like the first book, older kids and even adults will read it and love it. So run, do not walk, to your nearest book store and buy it. You will not be sorry.—Henry Chan*

Can you tell which is the news article and which is the blog? Here are some hints:

- News articles give factual information. They can announce new products or upcoming events. News articles are usually more formal. They should be objective, or not influenced by personal feelings.
- Blogs give ideas, views, and opinions on something. They may also include factual information, but the focus is on opinion. The writing in blogs is usually more informal. A blog is usually signed by the person who wrote it.

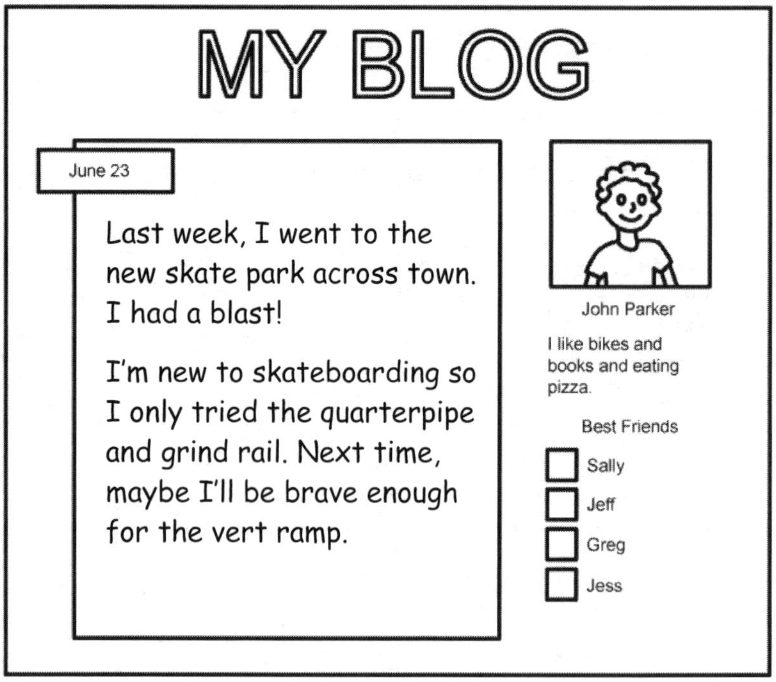

Why is it important to know about different forms of writing? The more you know, the more quickly you can find the information you want. If it is facts you are looking for, check a news article. If you want to know what different people think about something, check a blog.

"Blog or News?"—Think About It

1. Which item is a news article? Use information from the text to support your answer.

2. What are the similarities and differences between the news article and the blog? Explain fully.

3. What is the difference between formal and informal writing?

4. Would you write a news article or a blog for your school's website if you wanted to get people in your community to come to your school play? Use information from the text to help explain your thinking.

5. What is the main idea of this text? How does the author support this main idea? How does this help you as a reader?

6. What is the meaning of the word *sequel*? Use specific details from the text to support your answer.

How *Star Wars* Changed Moviemaking Forever

"May the force be with you!" If you are a *Star Wars* fan, then you have probably heard that phrase many times. If you are not a fan, you are still likely familiar with these words. So many characters, devices, and phrases from the movie have become well known. But you might be surprised to find out how much this science-fiction movie has changed how movies are made.

Special Effects

"A long time ago in a galaxy far, far away…" is how *Star Wars* begins. Its plot was not revolutionary. In fact, it was quite old-fashioned. The story was typical science fiction with lots of drama, corny characters and good battling evil, in space and in hand-to-hand combat.

It was the special effects that made *Star Wars* stand out from other movies. People still talk about the light sabers that hummed and slashed. Spaceships zoomed through space and landed on huge, realistic-looking space stations. Moviegoers had never seen anything like it.

Those incredible special effects were created on computers by a company headed by George Lucas, *Star Wars*' writer and director. That company continues to change moviemaking because it is still one of the top special-effects companies, using computer graphics to create many of the effects that you see in movies today.

Movie Theatres Expand

Star Wars was so popular that people flocked to movie theatres to watch it. Some returned to see it again and again. The movie quickly set box office records. Suddenly the owners of the movie theatres had lots of money.

When *Star Wars* first came out in 1977, most movie theatres were stand-alone buildings, with just one movie screen. Using the money the film had made for them, movie-theatre owners built more theatres, leading to the multiplexes that are common today.

Theatres needed more movies to show on all the additional movie screens and in all the new multiplexes. So new movie companies sprang up, including small organizations that created experimental movies trying out new techniques. Some of these methods became popular and some failed but, thanks to *Star Wars*, people got to see new types of movies.

How *Star Wars* Changed Moviemaking Forever (continued)

Another way *Star Wars* changed moviemaking is that it was one of the first modern special-effects blockbusters. Other moviemakers tried to copy it. It also was the first really successful movie trilogy. There had been movie sequels previously, but they were often just poor imitations of the first movie. The *Star Wars* movies were all popular. There have been two trilogies so far, with more planned.

Star Wars continues to influence and inspire people. Inventors have even tried to create some of the things you see in the movies, including the hologram images and the huge AT-AT robots.

Movie Robots Versus Real-Life Robots

Star Wars featured two memorable robots called R2-D2 and C-3PO. R2-D2 was a small, handy robot. It had tools stored in its body and could help to maintain and repair starships. It communicated using sounds such as beeps and whistles. C-3PO looked and behaved like a human. It was programmed to speak many languages so that it could help life forms from different planets communicate with each other.

Real-life robots are not as intelligent as robots in *Star Wars* or other movies. In real life, robots can do a few specific tasks. We have robots that can vacuum a room, assemble a car, explore the ocean, and search a disaster site, but none of these robots looks or behaves like a human.

Scientists are working to make robots smarter and more versatile. One of the most advanced humanoid robots is ASIMO. It can walk, run, turn smoothly, climb stairs, and understand simple voice commands. It can use its camera eyes to create a map of its environment and avoid obstacles that are in its way. Another humanoid robot, REEM-A, can hold objects and play chess. Scientists with the Nursebot project want to help older people live better. A Nursebot could remind people to do important things, such as take their medicine. It could help them open doors or cupboards if they have trouble using their arms and hands.

REEM-A the chess-playing robot

"How *Star Wars* Changed Moviemaking Forever"—Think About It

1. Have you seen any of the *Star Wars* movies? If so, which one is your favourite and why?

2. List two things that the *Star Wars* movies have done to help change moviemaking.

3. What sentence in the text tells us that *Star Wars* has inspired inventors to create new inventions?

4. Who is the director of the *Star Wars* movies?

5. What are the names of two robots from the *Star Wars* movies? What are the names of two real-life robots?

6. How are movie robots different from real-life robots? Use examples from the text to support your answer.

Camera Language

Creating a video is very easy today. You can shoot videos with video recorders, most digital cameras, and even smart phones. You can edit videos using programs on the Internet. And you can show your videos on your television or your computer.

If you want to make a good video, you will need to think creatively, and you will need to follow some basic steps. One of these steps is the making of a storyboard. Once you have the idea for your video and have written a script, it is time to make a storyboard. A storyboard is like a cartoon strip of what the video will show from beginning to end. Each frame, or box, shows a shot you want to take. In the frame, there is a rough drawing or sketch of the shot. What is happening in the shot is usually described in words. Sometimes what a character will say is included too. How the shot will be filmed is also explained. This is where you need to know camera language.

Here are some words that videographers and moviemakers use to describe shots. The same vocabulary is used whether you are making a three-hour movie or a video of your dog doing tricks. Some of these shots are effects created when editing.

- **Close-up Shot:** This means just what it says. It is a shot that is close to the subject of the shot. It is used to show details of the setting and emotions of the subject. A **long shot** means what it says too. It is a shot taken from a distance. It gives a wider view of the subject and shows more of the setting. A **medium shot** is a shot that would show a person from the waist up when they are sitting or standing.
- **High Camera Shot:** This is a shot that is taken from above the subject. It is sometimes used to make the subject appear weak by making it look small. A **level camera shot** is taken even with the subject. This is a very common shot. A **low camera shot** is taken looking up at the subject. Because this shot makes the subject look big, it can make the subject appear powerful.

Long shot of Christine riding to the boathouse.

- **Pan:** In this shot, the camera moves slowly across a scene in a sweeping movement. It is used to show the setting in more detail than a long shot.
- **Zoom In:** The shot starts away from the subject, then slowly moves closer. It is a way to focus the viewers' attention on what will be happening. **Zoom out** is the opposite—the camera moves out slowly from the subject.
- **Fade-out:** In a fade-out, the shot slowly fades to black. This is often used at the end of a film. A **fade-in** is the opposite—a shot slowly appears from a black screen. This is often used at the beginning of a film. In a **dissolve**, one shot fades out while another shot is fading in.

"Camera Language"—Think About It

1. What technology could you use today to make a video?

2. The author gives a list of the words used to describe shots. Which words in the list are in bold? How can this help you when reading?

3. How are the shots in a storyboard arranged?

4. When might you use a high camera shot? When might you use a low camera shot?

5. Why do you think the author included the second paragraph describing storyboards?

6. Which of the shots listed do you think would be done when editing? Why?

Phones on the Go

New Yorkers could not believe their eyes. There, out on the sidewalk, a man seemed to be making a phone call! The crowds walking by were amazed.

Today, no one would look twice at someone using his cell phone as he walked in the street. But back on April 3, 1973, it was an amazing sight. That is because it was the first cell phone call ever made.

One Heavy Little Phone

Scientists and engineers had been working for many years to create a phone that could be used anywhere and was not tethered by a cord. The biggest problem was making a power source that was not too heavy to carry. In the mid-1940s, engineers had built a mobile telephone that could be used in a car, but the phone weighed about as much as a 12-year-old child. Imagine carrying that phone around!

The phone that Martin Cooper used on the streets of New York in 1973 was a big improvement over those earlier, heavier phones. He had been working on the phone for some time and he knew he was in a race with other researchers to create the first cell phone that anyone could use anywhere. Cooper's first phone call on his cell phone was to his main rival, Joel Engel. "Joel, this is Marty," began that first-ever call. "I'm calling you from a cell phone, a real hand-held portable cell phone."

Cooper's phone weighed about 0.9 kilograms or about as much as a litre of milk. Compare that with how light a cell phone is today. As Cooper said, "The battery lifetime was 20 minutes, but that was not really a big problem because you could not hold that phone up for that long."

Keeping In Touch

The phone became known as a cell, or cellular, phone because the phone calls are transmitted over areas that are called cells. Cooper invented the device because he hoped it would make people safer, since they could always be in touch and call for help if they needed it. He also thought cell phones could bring people the freedom to work and communicate wherever they wanted.

But Cooper could not imagine how popular his invention would become. "We had no idea that in as little as 35 years more than half the people on Earth would have cellular telephones," he once said. He also did not foresee concepts such as Facebook and Twitter and how people use cell phones to communicate today.

There are now more than 5 billion cell phones in the world. People use them in many ways, including to find survivors in disasters, to access banks where they are scarce, and even to gather people to start revolutions.

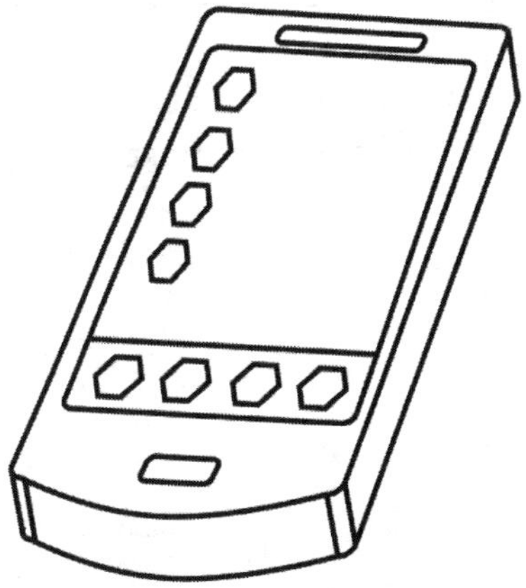

A smart phone is smaller and lighter than the first mobile telephones.

"Phones on the Go"—Think About It

1. Why do you think Martin Cooper's first call was to his rival?

2. Cell phones allow you to keep in touch with almost anyone at all times. Do you think this is a good idea? Why or why not?

3. What does the phrase "no one would look twice" mean? Does the author really mean that no one would look at a person using a cell phone twice, or does it have another meaning?

4. Martin Cooper said, "Technology makes your life better, more convenient, safer, educates you, entertains you, and mostly makes you more productive." Do you agree or disagree? Why?

"Phones on the Go"—Think About It (continued)

5. Martin Cooper also said, "The cellphone in the long range is going to be embedded under your skin behind your ear along with a very powerful computer who is in effect your slave." Do you agree? What do you think of this idea? How do you think most people will feel about it?

6. How do the subheadings in the text help you understand the information being given? How else could this information be organized using graphic organizers?

A **smartphone** is a cell phone that can do much more than make and receive phone calls. Many smartphones have keypads or touchscreens that you can use to write text messages and emails. They have screens on which you can watch videos, surf the Internet, or read articles. You can use a smartphone to take pictures, record a video, get directions, listen to music, or play games. Applications, or apps, let you use your smartphone as a flashlight, an alarm clock, a calculator, an address book, and a calendar.

The Computer Revolution

Today, everyone knows computers are machines that we depend on in countless ways every day. But did you know that back in the early 1600s people were already using the word *computer*? Back in those days, it meant someone who did calculations or computations. Computers have changed a lot since then.

The First Computer

Computers are machines that can be programmed to carry out sequences of logical or mathematical operations. Computer-like machines were first designed as long ago as the early 1800s, but none of them were ever built then.

Most experts agree that the first computer was not actually built until 1942. It was called the Atanasoff-Berry Computer, or ABC, after its American inventors, John Vincent Atanasoff and Clifford Berry. This computer could not be programmed, as computers today can be, but it was a start.

Scientists worked to make the computer programmable—this was the computer's software. But they also experimented to improve the actual machine, which was the computer's hardware. By 1946, they had created ENIAC, the first programmable computer. It could spit out results 1000 times faster than other machines of the time!

Scientists in England were working on improving computer software. In 1948, they created a computer they called Baby. It was the first computer that could store program instructions in its memory.

From Big to Little

One of the main ways that early computers differ from the ones you use today is that the old machines were huge. Computers such as ENIAC were more than twice as big as a classroom.

Computers had to be so big because they were powered by large glass tubes called vacuum tubes. Not only did these tubes become very hot when they were working, but they also did not work very well. Although there might be thousands of vacuum tubes in a single computer, if even just one burned out, then the entire computer would stop working.

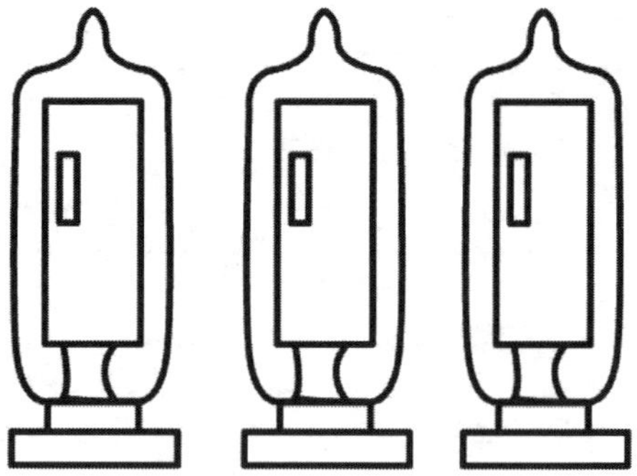

Vacuum tubes

That all changed in the late 1950s when transistors began replacing the vacuum tubes. Transistors are tiny devices that are used to increase and change electronic signals and electrical power. They are much smaller and lighter than vacuum tubes and are also cheaper to make, more durable, and much more reliable.

The Computer Revolution (continued)

Your Life with Computers

Thanks to transistors, computers became much smaller, more reliable, and more powerful. But scientists kept working to improve computers. They figured out how to put hundreds of transistors on an even smaller microchip. Suddenly computers became much smaller and much more powerful. Today, millions and even billions of transistors can be placed on a single microchip the size of your fingernail.

Without the computer, there would be no Internet, personal computers, or many other technologies. In fact, most machines you use today are powered by computers.

Fun Facts

- The original Atanasoff-Berry Computer (ABC) no longer exists. It was taken apart because it was too wide to fit through the door of the room it was built in. Between 1994 and 1997, engineers, scientists, and students worked together to build a reconstruction, or copy, of ABC so that they could learn more about how it worked.
- Transistors have made it possible to design and build portable computers. A portable computer is small enough and light enough to be carried around easily. The first truly portable computer came out in 1981. It weighed 11 kg and it looked like a small, plastic suitcase—it even had a handle! Today, laptop computers are much smaller and lighter. Some laptops weigh only about 1 kg.
- Most microchips today are made from silicon. Silicon is the main ingredient in beach sand.

"The Computer Revolution"—Think About It

1. What made early computers huge, and what makes them so much smaller today?

2. What are some advantages of having smaller computers?

3. Read the text again, then write two other possible titles for it.

4. a) List all the ways that you have used computers today.

b) Choose one way that you have used a computer and think about how you could have lived without it.

Cool As a Cucumber

Did you know the inside of a cucumber is often much cooler than its outside? No wonder that for hundreds of years, people have said someone is "cool as a cucumber" if the person stays calm no matter what is happening.

There are many expressions about food that people use to explain situations or pass along advice. Most people know what a cucumber is and that makes the phrase easy to understand and remember.

How many of these other food expressions do you know?

An Apple a Day Keeps the Doctor Away

Apples contain lots of vitamin C, clean your teeth, and keep you healthy in lots of other ways. Apples are very good for you. That is why parents sometimes encourage children to eat the fruit by saying it will cut back on visits to the doctor.

People have known for a long time that apples help keep you in top shape. This rhyming expression is a simplification of "Eat an apple on going to bed, and you'll keep the doctor from earning his bread."

The Big Cheese

No one knows for sure how "the big cheese" came to mean a very important person. About 150 years ago, "cheesy" meant anything that was first-rate, but today it means something that is cheap or corny.

Some people think the expression comes from the Persian or Hindi word *chiz*, which means "thing." About 100 years ago, the word "big" was added to describe wealth and power.

Couch Potato

If you have been sitting motionless watching television for a long time, has someone ever called you a couch potato? It means you are spending too much time doing nothing and you should get up and get some exercise.

Old televisions had tubes inside them and potatoes are a type of plant known as a tuber, so that is how the two became connected. Most people sit on a sofa or couch to watch Television, so that was added to the phrase. This expression has only been around since the mid-1970s.

There's No Use Crying Over Spilled Milk

This is another expression that people have used for hundreds of years, but no one remembers where if came from. Here is one suggestion: Spilling or wasting any food was a bad thing long ago when people had little to eat. But some families left out a gift for fairies or sprites and that treat was often cold, creamy milk. So spilling milk could be seen as a good thing since it could make the fairies happy and bring good luck. Besides, there was no point being upset over something that had already happened and could not be changed.

Here are more expressions and sayings that involve food. Which ones have you heard before and which ones are new to you? What do you think they mean?

As alike as two peas in a pod	Sour grapes
Bite off more than you can chew	Smart cookie
Cream of the crop	There is no such thing as a free lunch
Eat humble pie	You cannot make an omelette without breaking eggs
In a pickle	You are what you eat

"Cool As a Cucumber"—Think About It

1. What are some of the characteristics of a good, useful expression?

2. Write the sentence in the text that the expression "an apple a day keeps the doctor away" came from.

3. Why might the expression "the big cheese" not be related to the food cheese? What sentence in the text hints that there may be a different reason we use this expression?

4. Why do you think people come up with food expressions like the ones you have just read about?

5. What is the connection between a television and a potato? Write the sentence from the text that helps explain your answer.

6. Choose one of the expressions you have just learned. What does each part of the expression mean? What does the whole expression mean?

Science Fiction and Fantasy

Science fiction and fantasy novels are very popular forms of writing for people of all ages. Science fiction and fantasy are different genres. This means that all science fiction books have certain characteristics in common, and all fantasy books have characteristics in common.

Definition of Genre

A genre is a category of an artistic, musical, or literary creation. Each genre has a particular style, form, or content. So westerns are one genre of movies; hip-hop/rap is one genre of music; and biographies are one genre of literature.

Science Fiction

Science fiction stories often tell about science and technology of the future. The science and technology in these stories have some basis in actual science and fact. The stories should not be completely unbelievable. The settings for these stories are often in the future on Earth, in space, or on a different world. So the situations people in the story find themselves in are different than what could happen today.

Ender's Game by Orson Scott Card is a very popular science-fiction novel for young people (and adults too). The story takes place in the future on Earth. In it, a young boy (Ender) is chosen to go to a very special military school. There he trains for war by fighting mock battles in zero gravity using special technology. The hope is that Ender, or someone like him, will be the one who can lead the final fight against alien invaders.

Fantasy

In fantasy, things happen that could not happen in the real world. Magic is a large part of fantasy stories. Characters may have supernatural powers. Witches, wizards, superheroes, mythical creatures, talking animals, and ghosts are often characters in fantasies. Common themes in fantasies include battles between good and evil or greed and unselfishness. Fantasy stories are often about long journeys or quests. Sometimes the whole story is set in a fantasy world. Sometimes the story starts in the real world but moves to a fantasy world. And sometimes, magical and supernatural things are found in the real world.

The Neverending Story by Michael Ende is a popular fantasy story. In it, a young boy has just lost his mother. He starts to read a book and, through the book, is drawn into a doomed world called Fantastica. He can save this world but, only if he can reach the ruler of the country and give her a new name. In his travels, he meets dragons, giants, and other monsters.

"Science Fiction and Fantasy"—Think About It

1. Why is *Ender's Game* science fiction? Why is *The Neverending Story* fantasy?

2. What settings can a fantasy story take place in?

3. The author says that the science and technology in science fiction should have a basis in science today. What does this mean?

4. What are the two main topics in this text? What does the author do to provide information about these two topics?

5. How does the author provide the reader with a definition of the word *genre*? How else could the author have done this? Which way do you like best?

6. What do you think the word *mock* means? Use specific details from the text to support your answer.

Harry and Katniss

Harry Potter and Katniss Everdeen. If you do not know these names, then you might be living under a rock. These are the names of the two main characters in two of the most popular book series today—Harry Potter in the series of the same name, and Katniss Everdeen in *The Hunger Games*.

The Hunger Games is a science fiction trilogy written by Suzanne Collins. The seven Harry Potter books are fantasy novels written by J. K. Rowling. Together, these two series have sold over 100 million copies in hard cover and e-book formats, and have been translated into numerous languages. Both have been made into very successful movies.

Series books can be divided into categories according to the timeline of the books. In some series, the books stand alone. They can be read in any order. The main characters are the same, but the events of previous books do not play a large part in the books that follow. The Nancy Drew books are an example of this. In other series, the books should be read in the order they were written because what has happened before is very important in each book. Harry Potter books and *The Hunger Games* are series like these. In some series, books are written later that "jump back" in time. For example, in the *Chronicles of Narnia*, the fifth book in the series (*The Horse and His Boy*) takes place before the events of the first book.

Why do readers like series books? The most important reason is the characters. Readers care about the characters. They want to know what happens to the characters. They begin to think of the characters as friends. Also, series books can show character development. Over the series, readers get to know the characters deeply. They see how they change and grow. Harry Potter ages from 10 to 17 in the series of books (not including when he was a baby). So readers can see him change and mature from a pre-teen to an almost-adult.

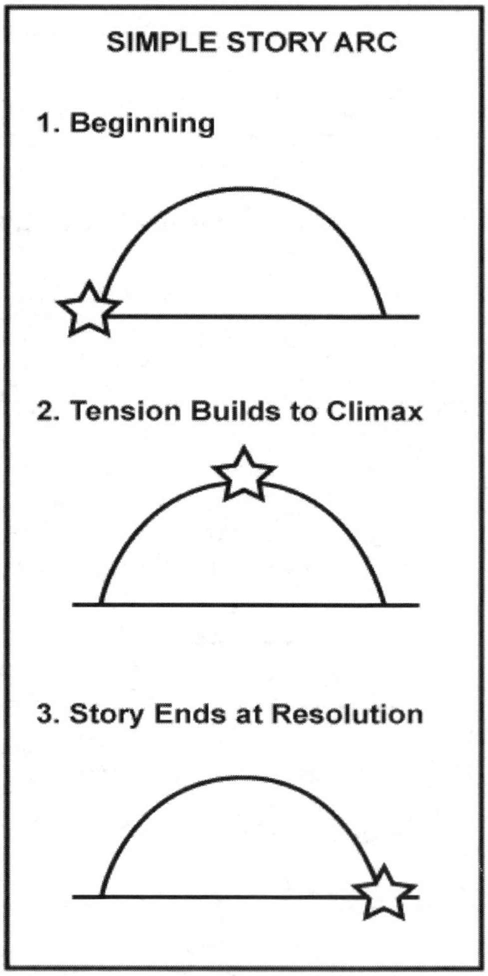

Another reason is the story arc. A story arc is the plot of a story. Most story arcs follow a similar pattern, which can be thought of as a mountain. In a series, there are two story arcs. Each book has a story arc. The ending of each book must be an ending to that book, but must also provide a link to the next book. The other story arc is for the series. Each book in the series moves the reader closer to the conclusion of the series. So to find out what happens at the very end, the reader must keep reading.

If you have never read a series, maybe it is time to try. You might just like it.

"Harry and Katniss"—Think About It

1. The author uses the phrase "you might be living under a rock." What does this phrase mean? How do you know?

2. There are no subheadings in this text. Where could you put subheadings? What could the subheadings be?

3. What is a stand-alone book in a series? Explain using information from the text to support your answer.

4. The author says that the two series are among the most popular books today. How does the author support this claim? Do you think the claim is true? Why or why not?

5. What are two reasons readers like series books?

6. How is the ending of a book in a series the same as the ending of a book that is not part of a series? How are they different?

The Magic Mirror

(Based on a folktale from Spain)

The king had decided that it was time to find a wife. At the palace, everyone was talking about the news. One of the servants asked, "How will the king choose his bride?"

"The king will not choose his bride," said the king's barber. "I will."

"You, a barber, will choose the king's wife?" the servant asked in disbelief.

"Indeed, it is true," said the barber. "I have told the king that I have in my possession a magic mirror. This mirror can see all the faults in a person's character. If someone has told lies or been unkind to others, the mirror can tell. If someone is greedy or too proud, the mirror can tell. It is impossible to hide anything from the mirror. For every fault, a dark spot appears on the mirror's surface. The king has agreed that I should use this mirror to choose him a wife. Any woman who wishes to marry the king must look into this mirror while I stand at her side. If no dark spots appear, she will become our queen."

"You are going to be very busy," said the palace cook. "Every unmarried woman in the kingdom will want to look into the mirror."

"Perhaps," said the barber, "but I will work night and day if necessary. Beginning next Monday, women may come to my shop if they are interested in marrying the king. I will have the mirror ready."

Soon everyone in the kingdom was talking about the barber's magic mirror. When Monday came, a large crowd gathered outside the barber's shop. Everyone wanted to see who came to look into the mirror, but not one woman entered the shop. The same thing happened day after day.

Each day, the king asked the barber if any women had come to look into the mirror. Each day he received the same answer—not one woman had come. The king became very discouraged.

"If I may make a suggestion," the barber told the king, "I have heard of a young woman who is said to have no faults whatsoever. She is highly praised by all who know her, but she is a poor peasant girl who spends her days tending sheep on the hillside. Would you consider marrying such a woman?"

"I would," said the king. "Tell this young woman about the mirror and see if she is willing to look into it. If she is, have her come to the palace. She will look into the mirror in front of the people in my court and anyone else who wishes to attend."

The next day, the barber led the peasant girl into the palace. The royal hall was filled with curious people who wanted to watch the event. The girl was very shy, as she had never dreamed of meeting the king, let alone marrying him. The king found her quite charming.

The Magic Mirror (continued)

"Has the barber explained to you about the mirror?" the king asked the girl.

"Yes, Your Majesty," she replied.

"You understand that if there are any faults in your character, the mirror will show them?" inquired the king.

"Yes, Your Majesty," answered the girl, blushing. "Everyone makes mistakes now and then, and I am no different. But I love and protect my sheep, and they seem to love me in return. I am not afraid to look into the mirror."

The king motioned to the barber to bring the mirror. The hall grew silent. The ladies of the court crowded around the young woman to see what would happen. They were sure she must have some faults. But when she held the mirror and looked into it, not a single dark spot appeared on its surface.

One of the ladies snatched the mirror and passed it around to her friends. No matter who looked into the mirror, no dark spots appeared. "It is a trick!" the ladies cried. "There is no magic in this mirror!" Many were furious that they—or their daughters—had missed a chance to become queen.

The king was not disturbed. "If you had been as confident about your character as this young woman, you would not have been afraid to look into the mirror," he said. "Perhaps there was no magic in the mirror, but it has found me a young woman who is worthy to be my bride."

"The Magic Mirror"—Think About It

1. Before the peasant girl came to the palace, no women wanted to enter the barber's shop to look into the mirror. In your own words, explain why.

2. After the barber described the peasant girl to the king, the barber asked him if he would consider marrying her. Why do you think the barber asked this question, if people said that the girl had "no faults whatsoever"?

3. a) Why do you think the barber lied about the mirror having magic powers?

b) The barber took a big risk by lying about the mirror. What could have gone wrong?

4. The mirror did not have magic powers, so it could not reveal whether the peasant girl had any faults. Why did the king feel confident that the peasant girl was worthy to be his bride?

The Wise Chief and His Wife

(Based on a folktale from Africa)

There was once a village with a very wise chief. All the people in the village brought their problems to him. This pleased the chief greatly. He was proud that the villagers respected his wisdom.

One day, an old man came to see the chief. "My four goats have been stolen!" he cried. "I am sure my neighbour did it. Please help me."

The chief sent for the neighbour. When he arrived, the chief asked him if he had stolen the goats. "Certainly not!" exclaimed the neighbour. "I would never steal."

The chief saw that this would be a difficult problem to solve, but this pleased him. Once again he would use his wisdom to find a solution and, once again, the villagers would be impressed by how wise he was.

The chief thought for a moment and said, "I will give you a question to answer." He turned to the old man. "If you give me the best answer, I will order your neighbour to give you four goats." Then he turned to the neighbour and said, "If you come up with the best answer, you may keep all your goats."

The old man and his neighbour agreed to the chief's plan. "Here is the question," announced the chief. "What is the fastest thing in the world? Do not come back until you have an answer. Do not ask anyone for help." The two men went home, scratching their heads and wondering what the best answer might be.

The old man could not think of an answer, so he asked the question to his daughter Shamika, who was both wise and beautiful. Right away, she came up with an answer. The old man was sure it was the best answer to the question.

The very next morning, the old man went to see the chief. "The question is not that difficult," the old man replied. "Time is the fastest thing in the world. It always goes too fast and we never have enough of it."

"Is this your own answer?" asked the chief. "If you lie, you will be punished."

The old man confessed. "My daughter Shamika helped me. She is very wise."

"Her answer is an excellent one," said the chief. "I would like to meet this daughter who is so very wise."

Soon after, the old man presented Shamika to the chief. The chief was impressed by both her wisdom and her beauty. He asked Shamika to marry him, and she accepted.

"There is one rule," said the chief. "You must not interfere with problems the villagers bring to me." The chief did not want people to think there was anyone in the village as wise as he was. "When we are married, everything in my house will be yours. But if you break this rule, I will send you back to your father."

The Wise Chief and His Wife (continued)

Shamika agreed, and soon after the two were married.

Before long, two boys in the village came to the chief with a problem. Each boy claimed that the other had stolen one of his sheep. Shamika could tell right away which boy was lying, but she said nothing. The chief gave them a question to answer, and sent them home to think. Shamika went to the boy who had told the truth and gave him an answer to the chief's question, even though she knew she should not.

The next morning, the boy told the chief the answer Shamika had given him. "Is this your own answer?" asked the chief. "If it is not, I will punish you."

The boy admitted that he had learned the answer from Shamika. The chief was furious. "I told you all that I have is yours," he said to Shamika, "yet you broke the one rule I gave you. You must return to your father's house."

Shamika asked if she could make the chief one final meal. "Fine," said the chief. "Then take whatever you want and leave my house."

Shamika prepared a huge feast of all the chief's favourite dishes. The chief ate until he could eat no more, and then he fell into a deep sleep.

With the help of some villagers, Shamika carried the sleeping chief to her father's house. When the chief woke, he demanded to know what was going on.

"You said I could take whatever I wanted," said Shamika. "The only thing I wanted was you."

"Where could I find a wife so loving and so wise?" said the chief. "You may return to my home with me. Only a fool would send you away, and I am much too wise to do that."

"The Wise Chief and His Wife"—Think About It

1. Why was the chief happy when the old man and his neighbour presented him with a difficult problem to solve? Give two reasons.

2. The chief was interested in meeting Shamika because she was wise. Why did the chief not want Shamika to display her wisdom by helping with the problems that the villagers brought to him?

3. a) Why did Shamika give one of the boys an answer to the question the chief asked, when by doing so she was breaking the chief's rule?

b) Think about your answer to the question above. What does it tell you about Shamika?

4. Who do you think is wiser—the chief or Shamika? Explain your answer.

Body Language: What Does It Mean?

Body language is how we communicate without words or sound (nonverbal communication). Some researchers think we communicate with body language between 50 and 70 percent of the time. That is a lot of nonverbal communication.

Experts who study body language agree that body language can tell us what someone is thinking or feeling. They also agree that there are general actions which have meanings that we can use to understand body language. Experts say interpreting body language is not an exact science; body language only gives clues. But interpreting the clues can be interesting.

Facial expressions are probably the first and best clues as to what a person is feeling, even if they are saying something different. So many emotions can be shown by the face, such as happiness, anger, fear, confusion, and surprise. And facial expressions are generally universal. This means they do not change much from culture to culture.

Your mouth alone can say a lot. Smiling is probably the best-known way you can communicate with your body, but a smile can mean different things. It may mean the person is happy, but it may also express false happiness or sarcasm. If the mouth is turned down, it may mean that the person is sad or even in pain. Pursed lips might show that the person is feeling distrustful or disgusted. Biting the lip might mean someone is worried or anxious.

Eyes can say a lot too. If a person looks directly into your eyes while having a conversation, this might mean that the person is interested and paying attention. But someone who stares at you for a long time may be threatening. Blinking can be a clue too. People who blink rapidly may be feeling uncomfortable.

Arms and legs can give us clues. Crossed arms might mean that the person is feeling defensive about something. Standing with hands on hips might show that the person is in control. A person who is rapidly tapping his or her fingers could be bored, impatient, or angry.

Posture is how we hold our bodies, and it can tell us a lot about a person. For example, if you are sitting up straight, this might mean that you are paying attention. If you are slumped in your chair or hunched over, you might be bored or you might not care what is happening around you.

You can use body language to better understand how someone else feels. You can also use it yourself to show how you are feeling. So if you want to show someone that you are interested in what they are saying, stand up straight, uncross those arms, and look directly into his or her eyes. That person will get the message.

"Body Language: What Does It Mean?"—Think About It

1. Use examples from the text to explain what body language a person might use if he or she was bored.

2. Why are facial expressions considered universal? Explain fully using an example.

3. What is *nonverbal communication*? What do you think *verbal* means? Why?

4. What claim does the author make about body language? How does the author support this claim? Do you think the claim is valid (reasonable)? Why or why not?

5. How could understanding body language help you make a good impression on someone? Use examples from the text and your own ideas to explain your thinking.

6. What do the experts mean when they say body language is not an exact science?

Galileo and His Telescope

You would see mountains, craters, and valleys if you looked at the Moon through a telescope. If you looked at the planet Jupiter, you would see its moons. Galileo was the first person to see these things through a telescope. Galileo was born in Italy in 1564. He lived and worked in Italy all his life.

Galileo did not invent the telescope. It was first made by a Dutch lensmaker. But Galileo improved the design so he was able to study the stars and planets closely. Some people call him the first astronomer. His first telescope magnified what he saw by about three times. Later he built one that magnified by 30 times.

As he studied the sky, Galileo found proof that the planets orbit around the Sun. He was not the first person to believe this, but he was the first to prove that it was true. People of that time believed that Earth was the centre of the universe and everything in space moved around Earth. Galileo got into trouble with the government and the church for saying that what they believed was wrong. He had to take back what he said or else he would have gone to jail.

Remembering Galileo

Today we call the four moons of Jupiter that Galileo discovered the Galilean moons. In 1990, NASA sent a spacecraft to Jupiter. They called this spacecraft *Galileo*.

More Than an Astronomer

Galileo was more than an astronomer. He was an inventor as well. He invented the first thermometer. His thermometer did not measure exact temperatures. But it did show if a temperature was higher or lower or the same as another temperature. He invented a compass that was used for aiming cannonballs shot out of a cannon. Later the compass was used to survey land. He invented a device that used a horse and buckets to raise water. This was used for irrigation.

Galileo thought about the world in a new way. Before Galileo, people did not run experiments or test out their ideas. It was enough just to think about ideas. Galileo wanted to test his ideas and see if they worked in the world. Galileo was one of the first real scientists.

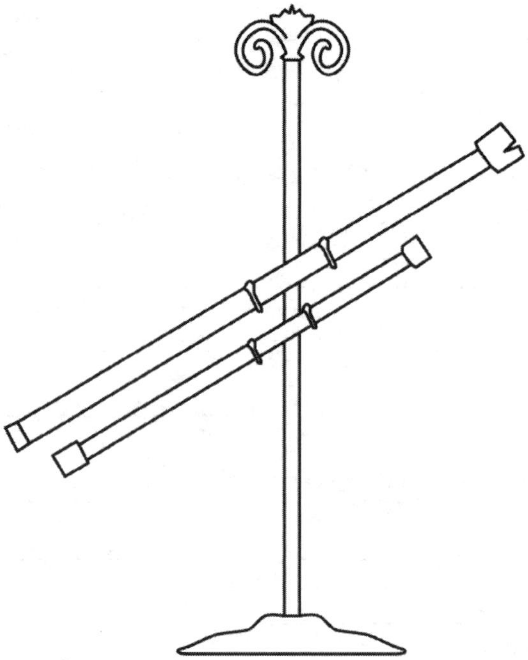

Galileo's telescope was called a spyglass

"Galileo and His Telescope"—Think About It

1. What did Galileo prove about Earth, the Sun, and the other planets? How did this get him in trouble?

2. One of Galileo's telescopes magnified 30 times. What does this mean?

3. How was Galileo's thermometer different from thermometers we use today?

4. Why do you think Galileo's telescope was called a *spyglass*?

5. The author says that Galileo was one of the first real scientists. How does the author prove this is true?

6. Write two or three sentences about the important things you learned about Galileo from this text.

Chris Hadfield

Chris Hadfield may be the most famous astronaut in the world today. His music video "Space Oddity," which he performed aboard the International Space Station, has made him a celebrity. But there is much more to Chris Hadfield than his singing.

Biography

Chris Hadfield was born August 29, 1959, in Sarnia, Ontario, and raised in Milton, Ontario. Chris is married to Helene Hadfield. They have three children.

Chris joined the Canadian Armed Forces in 1978. He became a fighter pilot, flying many types of aircraft for both Canada and the United States. During his time in the armed forces, he received a bachelor's degree in engineering in 1982 and a master's degree in aviation systems in 1992.

In 1992, Chris was selected as an astronaut by the Canadian Space Agency (CSA). He was one of four chosen from 5330 applicants. He was assigned to work at the National Aeronautics and Space Administration's (NASA) space centre in Houston, Texas. He also worked in the Russian Space Program as Director of Operations for NASA.

Chris has participated in three space missions. The first was in 1995 when he was a mission specialist on NASA's space shuttle mission to dock with the Russian space station *Mir*. He became the only Canadian ever to board the *Mir* space station. He was a mission specialist in 2001 on a mission to the International Space Station (ISS) where he helped install the Canadarm2, a new robotic arm. On this mission, he became the first Canadian to walk in space. In 2012, he travelled aboard the Russian *Soyuz* spacecraft to the ISS, where he stayed for five months.

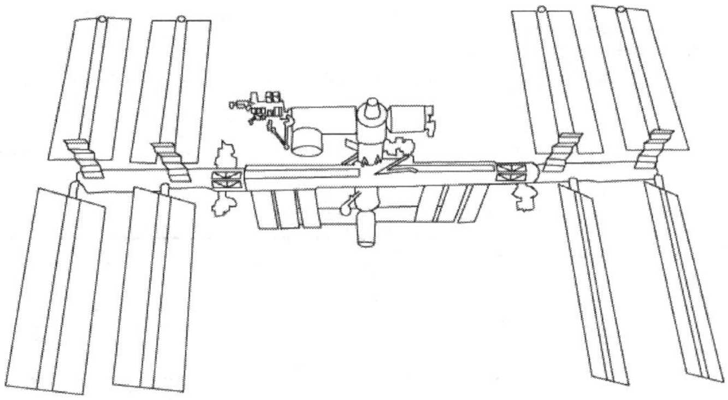

The International Space Station is the largest human-made object in space.

Chris retired from the Canadian Space Agency (CSA) in 2013. He has recently published a book called *An Astronaut's Guide to Life on Earth*. In the book, he describes his experiences in space and what he has learned about life by being an astronaut.

Chris has always been known for his enthusiasm. During his last mission to space, he commanded the ISS for the last few months of his stay. This is what he said before leaving on the mission: "To be able to command the space station, yes, it is professional, and yes, I'll take it seriously, and yes, it is important for Canada, but for me, as just a Canadian kid, it makes me want to shout and laugh and do cartwheels."

"Chris Hadfield"—Think About It

1. What "firsts" did Chris experience during his first two space flights?

2. What does the word *mission* mean in this text? Use specific details from the text to support your answer.

3. Acronyms and initialisms are abbreviations. An acronym is the first letters of a group of words that together are pronounced as a word. An initialism is the same as an acronym, only the letters are pronounced one at a time. Find three abbreviations in the text. Which one is an acronym? Which two are initialisms? How do you know?

4. How do you think the author feels about Chris Hadfield? Use specific details from the text to support your answer.

5. What is the purpose of the dates in the text?

6. Why do you think the author included the quote by Chris Hadfield? What does the quote tell you about him?

Wayne Gretzky

Wayne Gretzky is one of the most famous Canadian hockey players in North America. Even people who do not follow hockey know who he is. Gretzky played in the National Hockey League (NHL) from 1979 to 1999. He set many records during this time. Many of his records still stand today.

The Great One

Wayne Gretzky's nickname was "The Great One." How did he become so good? Wayne was two and a half when he started skating. A few years later, his father built a rink in their backyard. Wayne would practise four or five hours a day with his brothers. He and his brothers said they learned everything about playing hockey from their dad.

All the practising paid off. Wayne started playing in a hockey league when he was six. By the time he was 13, he had scored 1000 goals in the league games and tournaments he played.

Wayne was not very big or fast or strong. But he was very smart about hockey. He always seemed to know where the puck was on the ice and what it would do. He would make the right play at the right time. He was not a very fast skater but he was an agile skater. He could change direction in an instant without losing his balance or slowing down. He was a great passer. He would pass the puck to where he thought his teammates would be, not where they were. He was not a selfish player. The most important thing to him was for his team to win. So he would pass the puck to a teammate who had the best chance to score.

Wayne always played his best every game. When he was young, his dad told him he had to perform for the people who were watching. They came to see him play, so he must always be at his best. This was a lesson he never forgot.

After Hockey

After he finished playing hockey, Wayne became involved in many businesses. He donates some of the money he makes to the Wayne Gretzky Foundation. This Foundation helps youngsters all across North America play hockey. Wayne believes that playing hockey helps develop skills that young people need. He also supports many other charities, donating his time and money to help others.

"You miss 100% of the shots you do not take." – Wayne Gretzky

"Wayne Gretzky"—Think About It

1. Why is Wayne Gretzky famous?

2. What did Wayne do with his brothers? How do you think this helped him become a good hockey player?

3. What does *agile* mean in this text? Support your answer with details from the text.

4. How did Wayne help his teammates?

5. How does the author feel about Wayne Gretzky? How do you know?

6. Think about the quotation "You miss 100% of the shots you do not take." Is this quotation only about hockey? Explain what you think the quotation means in your own words.

"In Flanders Fields"

Every November 11, people in many countries buy poppies to show they remember brave soldiers and are proud of them. Do you know why the poppy is the symbol of Remembrance Day? It is because of a Canadian doctor who wrote the most famous war poem ever, "In Flanders Fields."

A Brave Doctor

By the time World War I began in Europe in 1914, John McCrae had been a doctor for many years and had already served in the South African (Boer) War. McCrae was born in Guelph, Ontario, in 1872 and had been writing poetry all his life.

By April 1915, McCrae was in an area of Belgium known as Flanders. The courageous doctor was in charge of a medical centre in the middle of the battle raging there. He tried to treat the injured men, but dead and wounded soldiers kept rolling down into his dugout operating station. McCrae barely had time to eat and sleep—there was not even time for him to change his clothes.

Death of a Friend

In early May, a good friend of McCrae's was shot and killed in battle. McCrae sadly buried his friend, but wanted to do something more. He could no longer help his friend or any of the other dead soldiers around him. But McCrae knew that if he wrote a poem about them, he could tell of their lives and perhaps it would help people remember them.

Looking around, McCrae saw the blood-red poppies blowing in the wind in a nearby cemetery. They inspired him to write "In Flanders Fields." But he did not think the poem was very good and threw it away!

Luckily, another officer found the poem and realized how great it was. He sent it to magazines and newspapers in England and it was published in December 1915. The poem was an immediate success and it inspired people around the world.

McCrae continued to care for wounded soldiers in Belgium and France. He worked very hard. But, in January 1918, he came down with pneumonia. By the end of the month, this quiet but famous soldier, doctor, and poet was dead.

Still Remembered

McCrae's poem raised soldiers' and civilians' spirits during World War I. Organizers in Canada hoped the poem would help raise $150 million to support soldiers and others, but it brought in almost three times that amount.

Every year, Remembrance Day is celebrated on November 11 at 11:00 a.m., because that is the date and time in 1918 when the agreement that finally ended World War I was signed. Poppies are mentioned in McCrae's famous poem and that is one of the main reasons why the flower was chosen as a symbol of remembrance.

IN FLANDERS FIELDS

In Flanders fields the poppies blow
Between the crosses, row on row,
That mark our place; and in the sky
The larks, still bravely singing, fly
Scarce heard amid the guns below.

We are the Dead. Short days ago,
We lived, felt dawn, saw sunset glow,
Loved, and were loved, and now we lie
In Flanders fields.

Take up our quarrel with the foe:
To you from failing hands we throw
The torch; be yours to hold it high.
If ye break faith with us who die
We shall not sleep, though poppies grow
In Flanders fields.

"'In Flanders Fields'"—Think About It

1. Why do you think "In Flanders Fields" was such a successful poem?

2. What is your favourite line in the poem? Explain what you like about this line.

3. What was John McCrae's role when he was stationed in Flanders during World War I?

4. John McCrae was very brave. How were some of the ways he showed his courage?

5. What do you think these lines from the poem mean:
To you from failing hands we throw
The torch; be yours to hold it high.

6. What do you think the word *lark* means? Use the poem to help determine the meaning.

Camp X

Just east of Toronto, Ontario, is a small town that had a big secret during World War II. Whitby, located on the shores of Lake Ontario, was home to Camp X, a training school for spies from Canada, Britain, and other countries fighting on the side of the Allied forces during the war.

While the conflict raged in Europe, the camp was top secret, since enemy spies would have loved to destroy it. But after World War II ended in 1945, people around the world uncovered the incredible story of Camp X.

"Intrepid"

The founder of Camp X was a businessman, inventor, and spy named William Stephenson. First, he set up a spy network in New York. The network's telegraph address was "Intrepid" (which means "bold and courageous") and that became Stephenson's code name.

Intrepid then set up Camp X on the site of an old farm. Hundreds of men and women trained at the camp, including Ian Fleming, who wrote the series of books about James Bond. Some people claim Fleming based Bond on Stephenson! Intrepid was one of the most famous spies of World War II. People say Intrepid was one of the most important people fighting for the Allies in World War II. He accomplished so much—yet had only a Grade 6 education.

Parachutes, Sabotage, and Disguises

At Camp X, spies were taught how to decipher (or break) enemy codes, forge (create fake) documents (it could cause confusion for the enemy), as well as sabotage experiments the German were conducting on atomic power. They learned how to shoot guns and explode bombs, kill enemies silently, and parachute jump. Radio operators were also trained here.

Spies had to be very fit, so they were constantly exercising and training. They also learned to survive with little food, read maps, create disguises, write secret messages, and do all the other things they would need to do in their dangerous work.

At Camp X, Stephenson also helped maintain a complex telecommunications centre called Hydra. It was located at Camp X because it was safe to code and decode messages there, far from the listening ears of enemy radio operators.

Camp X Today

Now you can visit a park where Camp X stood. You will see the craters where spies were trained to use explosives. You can also see the pathway used by the guards as they patrolled the camp and kept its secrets safe from prying eyes. You can also visit a monument dedicated to the brave men and women who trained and worked there.

Nearby is a museum about the spy school. There, you will see forged money from various European countries, a comb with a hidden compass, a suitcase radio, and much more.

"Camp X"—Think About It

1. Why was it so important that Camp X remain a secret during the war? Use evidence from the text to support your answer.

2. Why do you think the author mentioned that William Stephenson only had a Grade 6 education?

3. Look at the subheading Parachutes, Sabotage, and Disguises. How does this subheading make you feel about being a spy? If this subheading were placed on a poster advertising a spy job, would it convince you to try to become a spy?

4. List some words that can be used to describe spies.

5. William "Intrepid" Stephenson maintained Hydra, a sophisticated telecommunications centre. Why else do you think some people think he was so important?

6. How is Camp X today different from how it was during World War II?

How Fire Changed the World

No one knows for certain how or when people first discovered fire and learned to control it. Nevertheless, this was one discovery that undeniably changed the world.

Experts believe it was more than 400 000 years ago that an early human noticed lightning hitting a tree and setting it on fire. Or perhaps someone rubbed two rocks together and the sparks that flew out caused grass to start burning.

On the Move

Once people could warm themselves around fires, they could move to cooler climates. They also gradually lost their thick, heavy body hair, because they no longer needed it—fires could keep them warm.

Less body hair meant people could hunt in the hottest part of the day without overheating. This was an advantage because that is the time when furry animals sleep and so are easier to catch.

All Together Now

Thanks to the light that fire provided, people could stay up later than they used to. That gave them time to make tools, clothing, and other necessities. They also had time to tell stories and bond with each other.

Before fire was discovered, people slept high in trees. The warmth of the fire drew them around it, and they began to sleep in small groups huddled around the fire. This led to relationships with the other families and meant the people had to learn to tolerate each other.

Yum!

Experts also do not know when someone accidentally dropped some meat in a fire, then ate it. Perhaps this long-ago person was curious and placed the meat in the blaze on purpose. The result was people cooking additional types of foods.

Cooking transformed our ancestors' bodies. People's digestive tracts began to shrink because cooked food is easier to process than raw food. Cooked food is softer, so people's teeth became smaller. People became taller and bigger because they were getting more nutrients. Brains also got bigger and people began living longer.

Red Hot

People began to find more and more ways to use fire. Some artists used charred sticks (charcoal) to draw—some of the artwork they created on cave walls still exists. Potters discovered their clay pots became stronger when put in a fire to bake. Others used fire to melt metal and make jewellery, decorations, tools, and weapons.

Some farmers still use fire to burn fields and remove grasses so they can plant crops. Long ago, people also discovered that when they used fire to boil water, steam was produced. Beginning in the late 1700s, that steam was used to power steam engines, and people were soon building steamships and steam trains to get around.

Fire was definitely one hot discovery!

"How Fire Changed the World"—Think About It

1. What are two reasons people used to sit around fires? How are those reasons the same as the reasons we sit around fires today? How are they different?

2. The wheel was invented about 5500 years ago. List some of the ways the wheel has changed our lives and is used today.

3. Imagine eating cooked food for the first time. Write five sentences about what you would feel, think, and taste.

4. What are three advantages that humans gained by eating cooked food?

5. The discovery of fire also protected people from insects and wild animals. How do you think fire protects people in this way?

6. Fire changed the world in many good ways, but it can also be very destructive. Use a graphic organizer to list the pros and cons of fire.

Horses in North America

The ancestors of the modern horse lived in North America millions of years ago. Over thousands of years, they changed and became more and more like the horses we know today.

Scientists believe that these horses spread to Asia and Europe by travelling over a land bridge between modern-day Alaska and Siberia in Russia. (This land bridge no longer exists.) Horses continued to live in North America until about 10 000 years ago. Then they disappeared. No one knows why for sure, but it might have been because of disease or climate change.

Horses were reintroduced to North America by the Spaniards in the 1500s. The British and the French brought their own horses later. The first horses from France were brought in 1665. Many of the horses brought here escaped. They lived in wild herds, mostly on the Plains. By 1900, there were over 2 million horses running free.

Thousands of years ago, the Bering Land Bridge joined Asia to North America.

First Nations and the Horse

Before Europeans arrived, First Nations peoples lived by using what they had in their environment. For transportation, Woodland First Nations used birch bark canoes to travel the rivers and streams. The Haudenosaunee (say it like this: *hoe-dee-no-SHOW-nee*) were exceptional runners and could cover long distances in a very short time. The Plains First Nations travelled on foot with the help of dogs to carry their goods.

How did the horse change this? It did not change much for the Woodland First Nations and the Haudenosaunee. They did use horses but still relied mostly on their older ways. Maybe this was because they were not migratory and did not move far from their settlements. And navigating streams and rivers by canoe was still a much better way to travel through the thick forests.

But the horse changed the Plains First Nations way of life a lot. These people were migratory. They moved often looking for herds of buffalo and other animals to hunt. The peoples of the Plains First Nations became skilled riders and used horses for hunting, warfare, and travel. Life became much easier with the horse.

"Horses in North America"—Think About It

1. Why did horses disappear in North America about 10 000 years ago?

2. What is the connection between the horses that disappeared from North America over 10 000 years ago and the horses brought over by the Europeans?

3. What is the root word of *reintroduced*? What does this root word mean as used in this text? What does the prefix *re* mean? What does *reintroduced* mean?

4. The Woodland First Nations used birch bark canoes to travel. What does this tell you about where they lived?

5. How did the horse help the Plains First Nations? Use examples from the text to support your answer.

6. What information does the map give the reader?

The Women of the Haudenosaunee Confederacy

Five nations made up the original Haudenosaunee (say it like this: *hoe-dee-no-SHOW-nee*) Confederacy. They were the Mohawk, Oneida, Onondaga, Cayuga, and Seneca. The Confederacy was formed many, many years ago. It was formed so these nations could live in peace with each other. In 1714, the Tuscarora Nation joined the Confederacy. Each nation had its own chief and council. The Confederacy had a Grand Council to deal with matters that affected all the nations.

You may know about some of the Confederacy's famous leaders such as Peacemaker, Aiionwatcha (Hiawatha), and Joseph Brant. You may also know about the Great Law of Peace. This law provided a way to settle differences with thinking and negotiations rather than violence and warfare. But you may not know about the role of women in the Confederacy.

Women and the Clan System

In each nation, there were clans. A clan was like a family. Every person in a clan was related to everyone else in the clan because they shared a common female ancestor. The clan someone belonged to was passed down from mother to child. So when a woman married a man of a different clan, their children belonged to the mother's clan. But they would also be part of the father's family.

Clans in the Haudenosaunee Confederacy are **matrilineal**. *Matri* comes from the Latin word for "mother." *Lineal* means "a direct line."

Women also owned the land where crops were grown. They tended the crops. When a woman married, her husband moved into the house of his wife's family.

The Clan Mother was the leader of the clan. The Clan Mother was usually the oldest woman in the clan. She had the responsibility of choosing the chief of her clan and making sure he did a good job. It was also her task to make sure everyone in the clan was well fed.

The clan system is still part of the Haudenosaunee Confederacy today. Women still have strong roles. Property is inherited through women. The Clan Mothers still select chiefs and provide advice and guidance.

Clans and families lived in longhouses.

"The Women of the Haudenosaunee Confederacy" —Think About It

1. A confederacy is an agreement between people or groups for a common purpose. How does this relate to the Haudenosaunee Confederacy?

____

____

____

2. What did the Grand Council do? What do you think each nation's council did?

____

____

____

3. Why is *matrilineal* a good word to describe the Confederacy's clans?

____

____

____

4. Why was the Great Law of Peace important?

____

____

____

____

5. How is the clan system today the same as it was in the past?

____

____

____

6. What are the five nations that made up the original Haudenosaunee Confederacy?

____

____

First Nations Inventions

First Nations people were the first to farm North America, to travel around it, and to build a civilization here. Like people everywhere, they created inventions to make their lives easier. Many of these inventions are still used today.

Getting Around

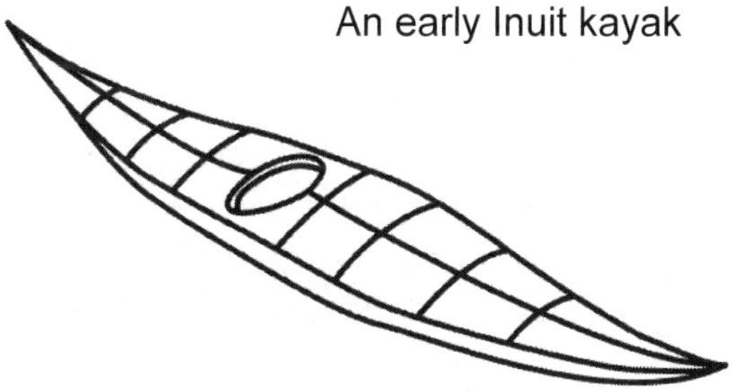

An early Inuit kayak

Inuit people needed a way to travel through the cold seas that surrounded them, so about 4000 years ago, they invented the kayak. The narrow boat is pointed at both ends and the paddle that propels it through the water has a blade on each end. Inventors have to use the materials that are available to them, so Inuit builders stretched seal skins over wooden or whalebone frames.

First Nations people near rivers and lakes created canoes to get around. Some used birch bark to cover the wooden frame, while First Nations people on the west coast created dugout canoes by hollowing out huge logs. First Nations people also invented the *travois*, a wooden frame for carrying food and other belongings that could be pulled by horses or dogs. And the snowshoes they created made winter travel faster and easier.

M-m-m-maple Syrup

Hundreds of years ago, First Nations people learned how to boil sap from sugar maple trees to make sweet syrup. Today people also make syrup from birch tree sap. Native people showed European settlers how to boil the syrup and pour it on snow to make maple syrup candy.

More importantly, First Nations people taught settlers how to make a tea from cedar bark and leaves. The drink was full of vitamin C and saved the lives of many explorers and pioneers. Native people also shared their secrets of freezing and drying some foods to keep them from spoiling.

Those Pesky Bugs

North America's forests are full of biting insects in the spring and summer, so it is no wonder that First Nations people invented ways to deal with them. They invented insect repellents using herbs, oils from cedar trees, a substance made from birch bark, and more. Using roots, leaves, and bark, they also created liquids and pastes to put on skin to take away the itch after the bite.

What Else?

You may think of sunglasses as being especially useful in the summer, but Inuit people originally invented them to prevent snow blindness in winter. The goggles they created were made from bone with a narrow slit cut in it to see through. These goggles reduced the amount of light that could enter the wearer's eyes.

First Nations created many other inventions, ranging from the game of lacrosse (it was originally called *baggattaway*) to diapers (they used soft, absorbent moss), and even the Jolly Jumper to entertain babies!

"First Nations Inventions"—Think About It

1. What features of the kayak make it suitable for travelling through icy, cold water? How do you think these features function?

2. The word *kayak* is a **palindrome**. This means it is spelled the same way backwards and forwards. List as many other palindromes as you can think of.

3. What are two things that First Nations people discovered could be done with maple sap?

4. There are four subheadings in this text. What is the main idea of the text below each subheading?

"First Nations Inventions"—Think About It (continued)

5. Many of the inventions listed in the text were created to help people get around. Why do you think it is important for people to be able to get around quickly and easily?

____

____

____

____

____

6. What is vitamin C? Where do you get get vitamin C in your diet? Why do you think it was important for First Nations people to find a way to get vitamin C in their diets?

____

____

____

____

____

____

7. Many First Nations inventions involve getting around. What would you like to invent to make getting to school easier?

____

____

____

____

____

____

____

____

____

____

Samuel de Champlain: The Father of New France

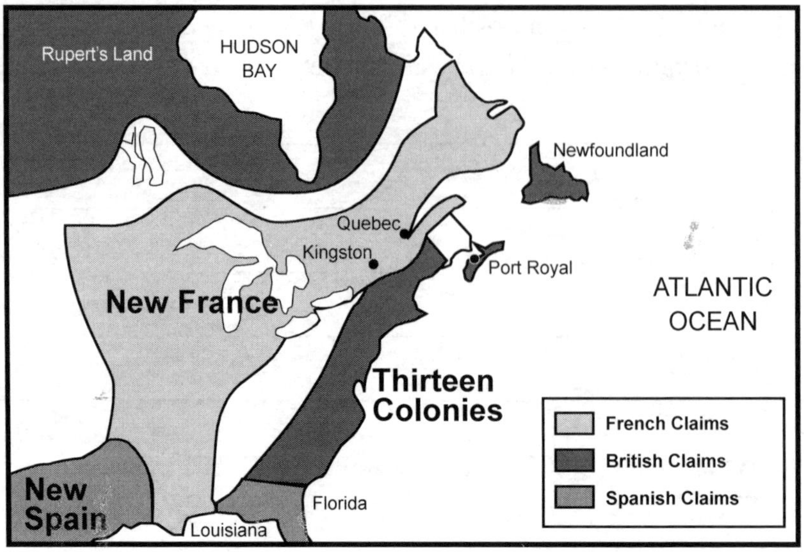

North America looked very different before Canada, the United States, and Mexico became countries. Starting in the 1500s, European explorers came to North America and claimed land for their countries. This map shows what land these countries claimed in the 1600s in the eastern part of North America.

Samuel de Champlain

Samuel de Champlain is called the Father of New France. This is because he explored and mapped much of the area. He also founded colonies. Later, he governed New France. Here are some highlights of Samuel de Champlain's life and accomplishments.

- Champlain is born around 1567 in France.
- 1599–1601: Champlain is part of a voyage to explore in the Caribbean.
- 1603: Champlain travels to North America as part of a fur-trading voyage. He maps the St. Lawrence River. He writes a book about his voyage when he returns to France.
- 1604: Champlain makes another trip to North America. He helps found a colony on Saint Croix Island.
- 1605: Champlain and the settlers move from Saint Croix Island to Port Royal. Champlain explores and maps the Atlantic coast down to Cape Cod. He returns to France in 1607.
- 1608: Champlain returns to New France and founds a colony that becomes Québec City. He forms an alliance with the Huron and Algonquin. He promises to help them with their fight against their enemy—the Iroquois. He discovers Lake Champlain.
- July, 1608: Champlain and his First Nations allies fight a battle with the Iroquois. Champlain and his allies win. The Iroquois become enemies of the French.
- 1612: Champlain is given powers by the French government to run New France. He continues exploring and mapping.
- 1615: Champlain is injured in an attack by the Iroquois. He spends the winter with the Huron and learns many things about how they live. He goes back to France after recovering.
- 1620: Champlain returns to New France. He does not explore anymore but spends his time governing New France.
- 1629: Québec City is captured by the British and Champlain is sent to England as a prisoner.
- 1633: Québec City is given back to the French and Champlain returns to New France to govern.
- 1635: Champlain dies in Québec City.

"Samuel de Champlain: The Father of New France" —Think About It

1. What did you learn about North America from the first paragraph? What did you learn from the map? Use your answers to write a summary of what North America was like in the 1600s.

2. How is this text organized? Do you think this is a good way to organize the information? Why or why not?

3. What do you think the word *accomplishments* means? How do you know? Support your answer with details from the text.

4. Find the words *alliance* and *allies* in the text. How are these words the same? How are they different?

5. Why did the French and the Iroquois become enemies? Support your answer with details from the text.

6. Champlain is called the Father of New France. What reasons does the author give for this? Include specific examples in your answer.

Fur Traders and Settlers in New France

Two groups of people who came to New France were fur traders and settlers. They came for different reasons, but both groups played an important part in the development of New France.

The Fur Traders

The fur trade was the economic start of New France. It was how people who came to New France made money. The fur traders had one goal: to get as many furs as they could. Beavers were the most important source of fur for them. Fur traders got their furs from First Nations peoples so they formed alliances, mostly with the Huron. This led to conflict later on with other First Nations peoples and the British. The traders also explored farther into the continent in search of more and better furs, so they helped open up new land.

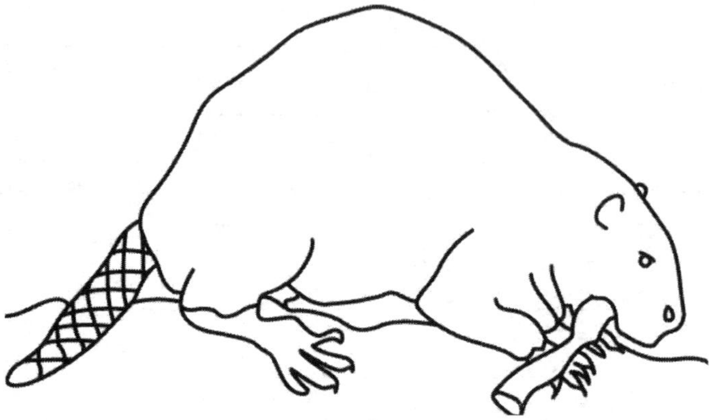

The beaver is the largest rodent in North America.

The fur trade caused changes in the way of life of the First Nations peoples. Before, First Nations peoples lived in harmony with nature. They took from the land and the animals only what they needed. Now they hunted animals to trade for goods from the fur traders. In some areas, certain animals were endangered.

The fur traders spent much of their time living with their First Nations allies. Many married First Nations women. Their children were the first of the Métis people.

The Settlers

The French first came to North America for fish, then for furs. Then they decided to build permanent settlements to help control the areas they were in. The French wanted settlements along the St. Lawrence River and around the Great Lakes. To do this, they needed settlers. The settlers who came were mostly farmers. Many of the settlers also worked in the fur trade to make money.

In the beginning, most of the settlers were single men. The king of France decided to send women to the new settlements. From 1663 to 1673, 1000 single women were sent. Many were orphans. They married as soon as they could and had as many children as possible. In this way, the population of New France grew. The women brought a dowry, or gift, of money from the king, and families were given extra money based on the number of children they had.

Life was hard for most of the settlers. They had to clear land, build homes, grow crops, and pay taxes. Diseases such as cholera and smallpox were common. But for most, life was better in New France than it would have been in France. By 1750, there were about 70,000 French people living along the St. Lawrence River.

"Fur Traders and Settlers in New France"—Think About It

1. What was the main reason fur traders came to New France? What was the main reason settlers came to New France? How were their lives different?

2. What did you learn about the women who were sent to New France by the king? Why do you think these women were chosen?

3. Some settlers worked in the fur trade to make money. Why do you think settlers chose to make money in this way?

4. What was the relationship between the fur traders and the First Nations peoples?

5. What changed for First Nations peoples after they started to trade for furs?

Old Money, New Money

It is hard to imagine there was once a time when money did not exist. But thousands of years ago, people traded, or bartered, with each other to get what they needed. For instance, if someone needed a cow, she might trade a few chickens for it.

But trading takes time, and it is difficult to move cows and chickens around for bartering. So people began using coins and pieces of paper to represent animals, food, and other items.

Salt, Feathers, and Whales' Teeth

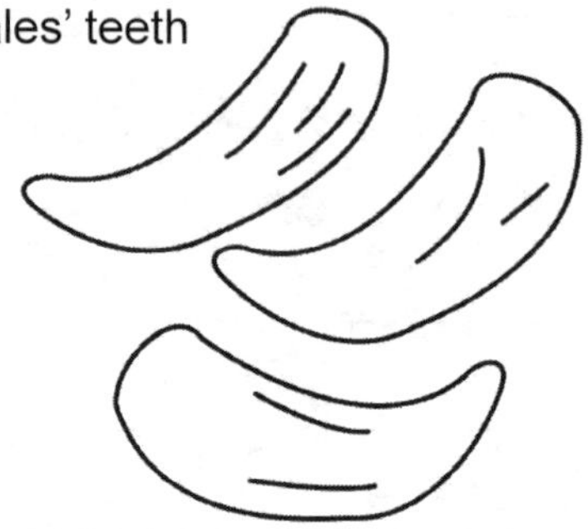

Metal coins have been used in various countries for money for about 3000 years. People started using paper money about 1000 years ago, because it was lighter to carry than coins.

Blankets, feathers, tea leaves, and even whales' teeth have also been used for money. Long ago in ancient Rome, workers were paid not with coins but with salt. That is where the word *salary* comes from. In Canada in the late 1600s, there was a shortage of coins so playing cards were used instead. The amount of money was written on the back of the card.

Some First Nations in North America used shell beads known as wampum for trade, in ceremonies for decoration, and to record agreements. It is hard to believe, but huge stone doughnuts were used as money by the people of Yap, which is an island in the Pacific Ocean. Some of the stones were so large they would not even fit in your bedroom!

Coins and Bills

People used to use 25¢ bills in Canada and the United States. These and other bills that were worth less than $1 were known across North America as *shinplasters* because they looked similar to a small, square piece of paper that was used at the time as a bandage.

Coins last longer than bills because metal is strong and durable. Money that lasts longer is less expensive to produce since it does not have to be replaced as frequently. That is good for the environment too. So many countries have switched from bills to coins for some of their money. Did you know that Canada used to have $1 and $2 bills? The government has even talked about changing the $5 bill to a coin!

Modern Money

Paper money may last as little as two years. That is why countries such as Canada and others are now printing polymer bills. They are stronger than paper and cleaner too, since they do not absorb liquid.

Countries are always looking for ways to make their bills difficult to counterfeit, or copy. Some bills have transparent sections, raised type, metallic images, holograms, and more. Other bills include Braille dots so visually impaired people can use them more easily.

"Old Money, New Money"—Think About It

1. Have you ever traded to get something? What did you trade?

2. Why do you think people stopped using large stone doughnuts as money?

3. If you are a "penny pincher," you are good at saving money. What do you think the expression "put your money where your mouth is" means?

4. Use evidence from the text to describe the advantages of using coins instead of paper money.

5. What changes do you think could be made to the coins or bills you use every day to make them more difficult to counterfeit and longer-lasting?

6. Money tells people about a country and the people who live there. On a separate piece of paper, design a $10 bill that represents you and your community.

The Pony Express

In the mid-1800s, there was no rapid way to get news across the United States. Ships carrying mail had to sail from the east coast of the country, down around the tip of South America, then up the west coast—and that trip could take six months.

Stagecoaches carried mail and news across the country, but it still took almost a month for them to go from one coast to the other. People began to wonder if there was a quicker way.

A Pony Express horse and rider

The First Ride

On April 3, 1860, a horseback rider galloped out of San Francisco, California. Over his saddle, Pony Express rider James Randall carried a *mochila* (you say it like this: *moe-CHEE-la*). In Spanish, the word means "backpack." It held the first mail that the Pony Express would carry across the country. The leather mochila could be slung on and off the saddle quickly. At each corner, the mochila had a locked pouch to carry the mail safely.

Randall had to find his way through heavy rains and slippery trails. About every 20 kilometres he stopped at a Pony Express station, where he leaped off his horse, flung the mochila onto the saddle of a new horse, hopped on, and continued riding. Each Pony Express rider switched horses on average five times before handing off the mochila to the next rider.

This relay system of horses and riders helped the mail move quickly across mountains, deserts, and swamps between San Francisco, California, in the west and St. Louis, Missouri, in the east. And while some riders were heading east on the Pony Express trails, other riders were heading west. The mail could travel 3164 kilometres in just 10 days.

Danger Ahead!

The first Pony Express trip almost ended in disaster. One of the riders was swept away by a rain-swollen river. He managed to scramble off his horse at the last minute—after grabbing the mail-filled mochila, of course. The horse was rescued and, with a fresh horse, the rider was soon on his way.

Raging rivers were just one of the problems Pony Express riders faced. Wild animals sometimes chased the horses, and riders had to watch out for poisonous snakes. Riders galloped through territory that Native Americans felt belonged to them, so they sometimes made the ride tough. Outlaws tried to steal the mochila. Sometimes riders had to detour long distances around damaged bridges or blocked trails.

End of the Trail

The Pony Express operated for only 18 months. By October 1861, telegraph lines had been strung across the continent. Suddenly news could travel in seconds, rather than days. But people have never forgotten the brave Pony Express riders and their horses.

"The Pony Express"—Think About It

1. Why do you think the Pony Express riders used a relay system?

2. Pony Express riders were brave. List the dangers they faced.

3. The Pony Express was replaced by the telegraph. What are some of the communications technologies that have replaced the telegraph?

4. How do people use horses today?

5. Summarize this text. Use the subheadings to help with your answer.

6. Imagine you are a Pony Express rider galloping across the plains, with no one else around and the next station still out of sight. Write five sentences about how you feel.

Mount Everest

Mount Everest is the tallest mountain in the world. At 8859 metres high, it towers over all the other mountains on Earth. Mount Everest is so huge that it even makes its own weather by changing the direction in which the wind and clouds move around it.

In Nepal, Mount Everest is called Sagarmatha, which means "Head of the Sky." In Tibet, the mountain's name is Chomolungma and that means Mother Goddess of the Earth. This incredible peak received the name Mount Everest in 1865. The mountain is named after Sir George Everest, a British man who was in charge of mapping the area and who was the first person to figure out exactly how tall Mount Everest is.

Climbing Mount Everest is difficult—and even deadly. One of the dangers on Mount Everest is altitude sickness, which makes climbers feel ill as they move higher. Altitude sickness is caused by the amount of oxygen in the air decreasing as people climb up the mountain. Symptoms of altitude sickness include headaches, lack of energy, joint pain, and other problems that make climbing especially tough.

Even at Base Camp, at the bottom of the mountain, where climbing groups gather and keep most of their equipment, some people really suffer from the low level of oxygen. Many climbers have made it to the top of Everest, but have not had the energy or ability to focus to make it safely back down.

There are lots of other dangers to climbers on Everest. Avalanches can sweep down the mountain almost daily. Blizzards and high winds threaten to blow climbers off the mountain.

It would be almost impossible to climb Mount Everest without the help of Sherpas, the people who live in the mountains near Everest. Because their ancestors have lived in the high altitude of the area for hundreds of years, their blood has extra red blood cells. That allows the cells to carry more oxygen than other people's cells can carry. That is a big advantage in Mount Everest's low-oxygen conditions.

Sherpas are excellent climbers and have incredible energy and strength. They are often hired by climbing expeditions to carry equipment and supplies. For the Sherpas, Everest is a very special and sacred place.

People had been trying to get to the top of Everest since the 1920s. On May 29, 1953, New Zealander Edmund Hillary and Sherpa Tenzing Norgay reached the summit of Mount Everest and made it back down again safely for the first time.

Mount Everest has been climbed about 6000 times but hundreds of people have died trying to make it to the top of this legendary peak. Even people who are not mountain climbers continue to be fascinated by this incredible mountain.

"Mount Everest"—Think About It

1. What are three possible dangers a climber might face when trying to climb Mount Everest?

2. Who were the first people to make it all the way to the summit and safely back to the bottom of Mount Everest?

3. What do you think the word *summit* means? Support your answer with details from the text.

4. Why do you think people in Nepal and Tibet chose names meaning "Head of the Sky" and "Mother Goddess of the Earth" for Mount Everest?

5. Sherpa climbers are known as "Tigers of the Snow." Why do you think they have that nickname?

6. Use a graphic organizer to list the advantages and disadvantages of climbing Mount Everest.

The Great Wall of China

It is the longest structure ever built anywhere in the world. The Great Wall of China is so long that, if you add together all its branches and portions, it would stretch from the North Pole down past the tip of Florida.

Construction on the wall began about 2500 years ago. Rulers in China's northern states wanted to mark the boundaries of their territories. They also wanted to keep out invaders from Mongolia. But the wall at that point was actually a series of unconnected walls, so it was easy for the attackers to just go around the sections.

Around 221 BCE, China's states were joined into one country. That was also when the sections of the wall began to be linked into one long structure. Building the wall was a difficult job that took many years.

Building the Great Wall

An ancient method called *hang-tu* or "pounded earth" was used to construct the Great Wall. For each section, a wood or bamboo frame was built. Soil was poured into the frame and packed down. Then another thin layer of soil was poured into the frame and pounded down. As the layers continued, the wall grew higher.

Soon the wall section was tall enough that workers had to carry their baskets of soil up ladders, then dump them into the frame. When the section was finished, the frame was removed, moved to a new part of the wall, and reused.

Graceful arches frame the Great Wall's doorways and windows as the long structure flows across mountains, plains, grasslands, and deserts with elegant twists and curves. Detailed carvings decorate the wall and its towers and gates.

The Great Wall Today

The Great Wall was renovated about 500 or 600 years ago to resemble what we see in modern times. In some areas the wall is as tall as three storeys and is wide enough that 10 people could walk along it side by side. Long ago, the wall was threatened by attacks from enemy warriors. But now it is threatened by sandstorms that have buried portions, and winds that wear away and erode the wall.

When the Great Wall was built, the Chinese believed there was no culture more important than theirs. Not only did the wall keep other people out, it also isolated the Chinese from the rest of the world. So Chinese culture developed with little influence from other countries. Inventions and discoveries made in China were secret and unknown outside of the country.

Today, the Great Wall does not separate China from other countries. Instead, it brings tourists from around the world to see this incredible structure.

"The Great Wall of China"—Think About It

1. Using examples from the text, describe the term *hang-tu*.

____

____

2. Use a graphic organizer to list the ways that the process of building the Great Wall of China would be different or similar today than it was 2500 years ago.

3. Why would a wall not separate or protect a country today the way it once could?

____

____

____

4. What is the main idea of the text under the subheading The Great Wall Today?

____

____

____

5. List three ways the Great Wall was decorated.

____

____

____

William's Windmill

For the majority of young people, being forced to drop out of school is the end of their education. For William Kamkwamba, it was just the beginning of his inspiring journey to becoming an inventor and author.

School Dropout

William is from the African country of Malawi, where families must pay tuition fees to educate their children. William's family was relatively poor and relied mostly on farming to make a living. Unfortunately, during a devastating famine in 2002, they were no longer able to afford to send him to school. So in 2002, when William was 14 years old, he was forced to drop out. Although he was disappointed, instead of becoming angry, he was determined to succeed and to be productive.

A Problem to Solve

The village of Masitala where William lived was very small and had no electricity. William's family used candles for light, but the candle smoke made his sister choke. William did not like hearing his sister cough so painfully and he began to wonder if he could do anything about it.

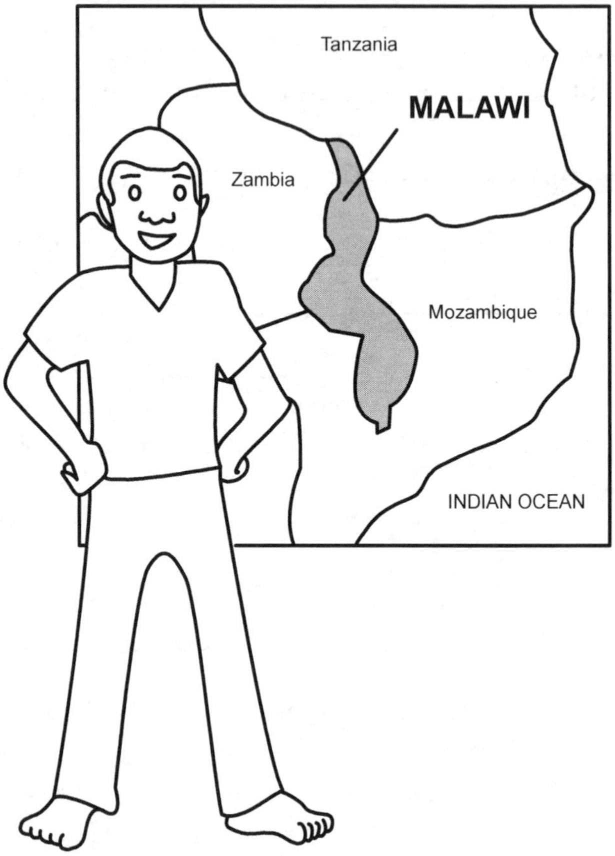

Finding Inspiration in a Book

William made frequent trips to the nearby local library. There, a picture of a windmill in a book about energy caught his eye. Winds sometimes blew strongly through his village, so there was plenty of wind power. But what could he use to build a windmill?

Using the rough plans William found in a book, he gathered whatever materials he could find, including scrap wood, a broken bicycle, a tractor fan blade, and an old shock absorber. He used the wood to build a tower, then he began experimenting.

The Windmill Takes Shape

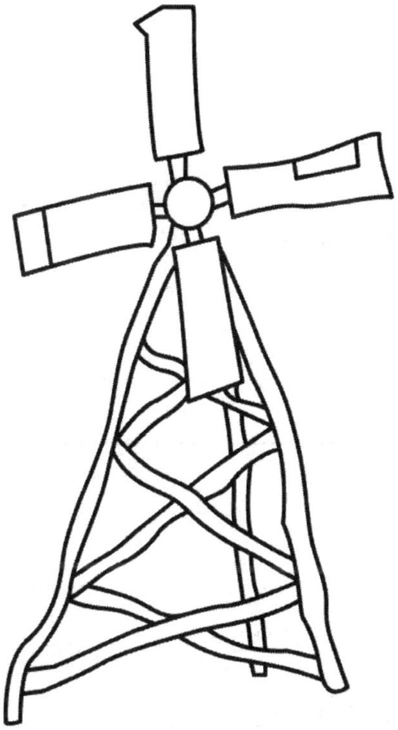

It was a challenge for William to find the parts he required, so he had to construct them. To build propeller blades for the windmill, for instance, he cut pieces of hard plastic pipe, heated them, then pounded them flat.

William was determined to stick with it—even when neighbours laughed at him. "All of these people were mocking me that I was going mad," says William, "but I had confidence in what I was doing."

Finally William thought his windmill was finished. Using wire, he hooked up the windmill to a small light bulb in his bedroom. William waited breathlessly for the wind to begin turning the blades. The blades started to whirl around and William saw the light bulb in his room glowing. He had succeeded! The windmill he built was able to power four lights and two radios in his family home.

Word Gets Around

William's village was proud of the young builder, and grateful too—his windmill generated enough energy that they could charge their batteries. One of Malawi's top educators visited William and soon returned with journalists. William rapidly became famous and was asked to speak at conferences around the world.

Thanks to his windmill, William has been the subject of a documentary movie and has a written book about his inspiring work. What is probably most important to William is that he was able to return to school. He even attended a university in the United States. All this because of a windmill and some determination.

In an interview in 2009, William was asked how he stayed focused on his windmill even while people were calling him crazy. This was his answer: "To encourage myself, I would look at the picture of the windmill in the book, and I would tell myself, 'Somewhere, someone did this thing. If somebody did this thing, I can also do it.' Even then, with people saying I was crazy, I'd say, 'OK, say what you are going to say, but I'm still going to do this thing.' I would not accept to stop doing this thing because of what people were saying."

"William's Windmill"—Think About It

1. List the ways William's life has changed since he created his windmill.

____

____

____

2. What does the text under the subheading School Dropout tell you about William?

____

____

____

3. Why do you think the other villagers laughed at William when he began building his windmill?

____

____

4. William is called a "Cheetah" in Africa. That means he is a strong person who does not wait for someone to help him solve his problems. Why do you think this animal is used to describe people like William?

____

____

5. How do you think William felt when the wind first began turning his windmill's blades and the light bulb went on?

____

____

6. William said, "I want to be an engineer, so I can make different things that make the world a better place, starting with my village." What would you like to do to make your neighbourhood or the world a better place?

____

____

____

What Is in a Symbol?

A symbol is something that stands for or represents something else. Symbols are often used to represent an idea. They are also used to represent places, such as a city or a country. Most countries have national symbols. These symbols are chosen to show something important about a country. Countries can have more than one symbol. For example, a country may have a national animal, a national plant, and national colours.

Most animal symbols are easy to understand. The dragon is the national symbol of China. India has a tiger as its symbol. New Zealand has the kiwi bird. So how do national symbols such as these get chosen?

Eagle or Wild Turkey?

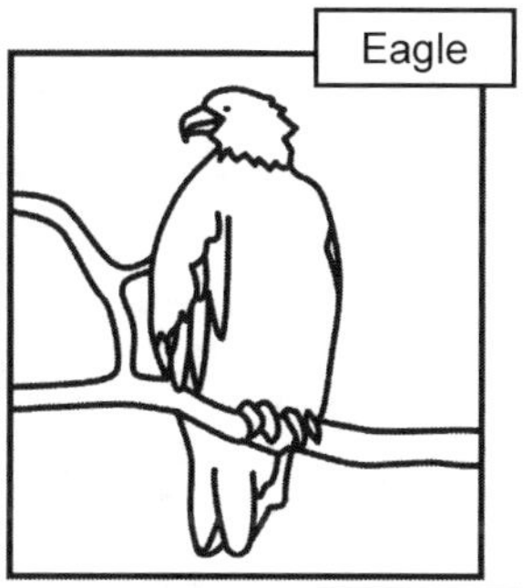

In 1787, the bald eagle was officially adopted by the United States as a national symbol. The bald eagle may seem to be a good choice. It was chosen because of its strength, long life, and majestic looks. It represents freedom, which is a strong belief of the country. But not everyone agreed with choosing the bald eagle.

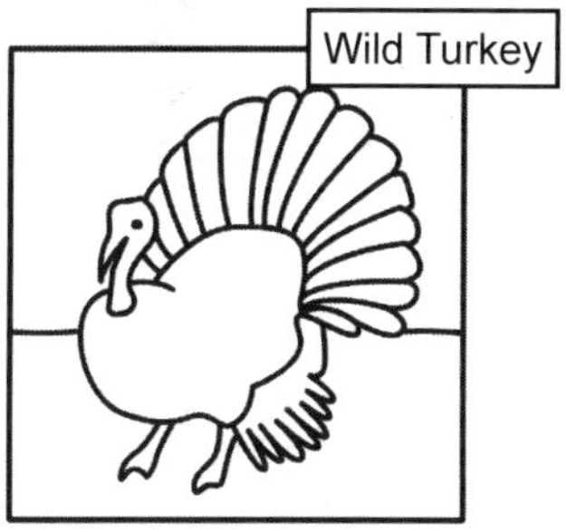

Benjamin Franklin (a Founding Father of the United States) wrote: "I wish that the bald eagle had not been chosen as the representative of our country; he is a bird of bad moral character; he does not get his living honestly; you may have seen him perched on some dead tree, where, too lazy to fish for himself, he watches the labor of the fishing-hawk; and, when that diligent bird has at length taken a fish,... the bald eagle pursues him, and takes it from him.... For in truth, the turkey is in comparison a much more respectable bird, and withal a true original native of America."

Beaver or...?

The beaver has been used as a symbol of Canada since the beginning of the fur trade. It has been used by companies, railroads, towns, and newspapers. The beaver, more than anything else, was responsible for the beginning and growth of Canada. The beaver was made an official symbol of Canada in 1975.

Some people think the beaver is a great symbol. David Morrison of the Canadian Museum of Civilization said: "I'm a big fan of the symbol of the beaver because I feel a country gets the animal it deserves. A beaver is an unaggressive, hard-working, waterproof, unassuming, wonderful animal and I think it speaks well of Canadians that we chose it."

Others think the beaver is too boring and would rather have an animal more majestic than a big rodent, such as a polar bear. Others think that the moose or the Canada goose is more of a symbol of Canada than the beaver.

"What Is in a Symbol?"—Think About It

1. What can a symbol represent? What is a national symbol?

2. What do you think the word *majestic* means? Support your answer with details from the text.

3. Benjamin Franklin wrote in the language of his day—in the 1700s. Read what he wrote. Summarize what he said in your own words.

4. What kind of animal is the beaver?

5. What was the main reason the beaver was chosen as a symbol of Canada?

6. What does David Morrison say about symbols and the countries they represent? What is the connection between the qualities of the beaver he describes and Canadians?

Morse Code

A hundred years ago, it was difficult for people to communicate over long distances. Messages to far-off places were carried on horseback. Then Samuel Morse invented the electric telegraph and the code it uses. The electric telegraph could send messages using electricity. The operator at one end used a machine to tap out a special code for each letter of the alphabet. The system changed the tapping into electrical impulses and sent them across electric wires to their destination. These impulses were changed back into the code at the destination. The code was printed on a paper tape attached to another machine. The operator on the receiving end used the code to change the message back into words. Later, operators learned to translate the code just by listening.

> The first telegraph message was sent in the United States in 1844. Canada followed in 1846.

Morse code is a series of dots and dashes. The dashes are about three times longer than the dots. Here is the code for the letters of the alphabet.

A •–	G ––•	M ––	T –
B –•••	H ••••	N –•	U ••–
C –•–•	I ••	O –––	V •••–
D –••	J •–––	P •––•	W •––
E •	K –•–	Q ––•–	X –••–
F ••–•	L •–••	R •–•	Y –•––
		S •••	Z ––••

The Morse code also includes codes for numbers and punctuation signs. Like texting, it also has groups of letters that stand for phrases. For example, the letters CUL stand for "see you later." And the famous SOS distress signal stands for "save our souls." Messages can be sent by Morse code using light too. A flashing light can send the same dots and dashes and they can be translated by someone watching.

How Is Morse Code Used Today?

Today Morse code is used mostly by amateur radio operators. Contests are held all over the world where these operators can show their skills in using Morse code. Some navigation beacons still identify themselves using Morse code. Pilots flying planes by instrument use these beacons to determine their plane's location. But perhaps the most exciting use of Morse code is helping people with disabilities communicate. There have been cases in which people have learned to communicate using their eyelids to blink messages using Morse code. Or they have used a finger to tap out messages.

"Morse Code"—Think About It

1. Practise using Morse code.

a) Translate this code into words. (The slash line means the end of a word.)

-- --- .-. ... . / ______________________

-.-. --- -.. . / .. ... / ______________________

. .- ... -.-- / - --- / ______________________

..- -. -.. . .-. ______________________

... - .- -. -.. / ______________________

b) Translate this sentence from words into code. (Use a vertical line to show the end of a word.)

I like reading about new ideas.

2. What was needed between two operators so they could send and receive messages?

____

____

3. Where and when do you think it might be useful to send Morse code messages using light?

____

____

4. What does the word *destination* mean? Use specific details from the text to support your answer.

____

____

5. The SOS distress signal stands for "save our souls." What does this phrase mean?

____

6. Is this text fact or fiction? How do you know?

____

____

Penicillin Saves the World

Alexander Fleming was a brilliant scientist—but he was also a messy one. So when he left his lab for a holiday in August 1928, he did not clean up the samples of bacteria he was growing. Fleming did not discover the results of his untidiness until he returned to work on September 3. What he saw changed the world.

Alexander Fleming

An Incredible Discovery

When Fleming entered his lab, he realized he had left one of his bacteria samples open. Mould had dropped onto the sample and contaminated it. That meant Fleming would have to begin all over again. He picked up the sample to throw it away. But then he stopped and took a second look.

To his amazement, Fleming saw that where the mould had landed on the sample, it had killed the bacteria around it. The scientist was curious about how it did this. Fleming knew that more than 500 years ago, some doctors and healers had applied mouldy bread to wounds to help them heal. Sometimes it helped, but the healers did not know why.

Fleming was determined to find out more about his fascinating mould. He grew a sample of it and discovered that it gave off a bacteria-killing substance. He called the liquid "mould juice" at first. Then, after a few months, he named it penicillin after the Penicillin mould that created it.

Penicillin at Work

Penicillin was one of the first bacteria killers, or antibiotics, that scientists ever discovered and it changed the world of medicine. During World War I (1914–1918), Fleming had worked in hospitals on the battlefields in France. He had seen soldiers die of wounds that had become infected. Fleming was well aware of how helpful a drug that killed bacteria could be and how many lives it could save.

By the 1940s, scientists figured out how to mass-produce penicillin, which meant it was soon available around the world to many patients. Doctors used the drug to treat diseases that had affected people for many thousands of years. Illnesses such as gangrene (the death of tissue caused by poor circulation) and tuberculosis (a disease of the lungs) could finally be effectively battled.

The success of penicillin encouraged doctors to experiment and find similar drugs and more types of antibiotics that could be used to treat other infections. Today, drug companies have figured out how to make synthetic penicillin, which makes the drug even more available to a wider group of patients.

It is estimated that penicillin and other antibiotics have saves the lives of more than 200 million people over the years. It is hard to believe it all started with a messy lab and an observant scientist.

"Penicillin Saves the World"—Think About It

1. How do you think Fleming felt when he first saw how the mould had destroyed the bacteria around it?

2. Create another title for this text and explain your choice.

3. Thanks to penicillin, doctors could cure diseases that had infected people for thousands of years. How do you think the doctors felt when they could successfully treat patients?

4. Fleming called his discovery "mould juice" and later, penicillin. What would you have called it? Use an example from the text to support your answer.

5. Fleming's discovery changed the world and saved millions of lives. Why do you think few people know his name?

6. Alexander Fleming said, "One sometimes finds what one is not looking for." What do you think this means?

How Compasses Changed the World

The compass was invented more than 2000 years ago. But it took more than 1000 years before it was used for finding directions and navigation. But a compass is a device that shows people where magnetic north is! So why was it invented if not for navigation? How was it first used?

Marvellous Magnets

An early form of the compass was created by Chinese inventors around 250 BCE. They used the device to help them align buildings and furniture according to the environment and forces of nature. This technique is called feng shui (you say it like this: *foong schway*) and is still used today.

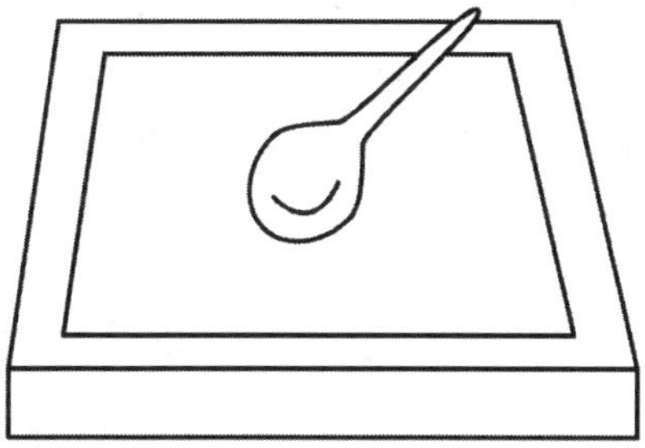

An early lodestone compass

These early compasses were built using lodestone, which is a mineral that lines up with Earth's magnetic field. Some experts believe the ancient Olmec people of Mexico might have used lodestones in a similar way to the Chinese, but 750 years earlier.

Eventually, someone realized that the lodestones were better at showing real directions, and that led to them being used as compasses. The pointing needle was a spoon-shaped piece of lodestone, set on a stone slab marked with some constellations and the points of the compass (north, south, east, west, and points between them). The handle of the spoon always pointed south.

> No one knows exactly how or when the magnetic properties of lodestone were discovered. According to one story, an ancient Greek shepherd named Magnes noticed that the iron nails in his boots and the iron tip of his staff were "sticking" to the rock he was walking on. That rock contained lodestone.

The Compass Takes Off

More than 1200 years ago, people figured out how to magnetize iron needles and these replaced the lodestone. These newer compasses were more accurate and portable, and could finally begin to be used by travellers and explorers.

A modern compass

How Compasses Changed the World (continued)

Before they had compasses, people navigated by the position of the Sun during the day and the movement of the stars at night. Obviously, this did not work very well in stormy weather or when clouds filled the sky. Sailors had to keep the shore in sight so they could see landmarks, or they risked getting lost.

Compasses made it possible for explorers to sail far out into oceans and away from land—no matter what the weather was like. This led to more exploration, the discovery of new countries, and trade with other cultures. Compasses also helped ships stay on course, which was important for explorers who were trying to return home.

Compasses in Modern Times

The world-famous scientist Albert Einstein often spoke about how he had been fascinated by compasses when he was a little boy. The movement of the needle amazed him, and he and other scientists investigated magnetism, which has led to many scientific discoveries.

Although many people still use compasses, in the late 1900s, people began using the Global Positioning System (GPS) to get around. It uses position and time information from satellites circling Earth to provide directions.

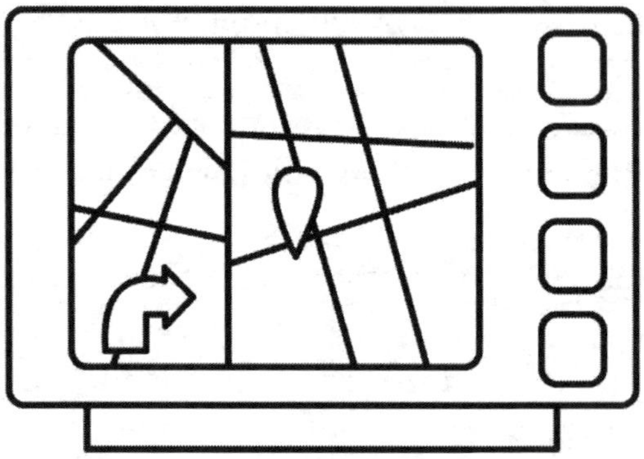

A GPS system in your car can give you up-to-date maps and directions.

Fun Facts

- The four main points marked on a compass—north, south, east, west—are called *cardinal points.*
- A modern hand-held compass uses a magnetized needle inside a small container filled with fluid. The fluid is often oil, kerosene, or alcohol. The fluid helps the needle remain steady.
- During World War II, British pilots carried secret tools that they could use to escape if they were captured. The tools were hidden in everyday objects. Small compasses were hidden in boots, pens, and even buttons!

"How Compasses Changed the World"—Think About It

1. The word *compass* comes from an old word meaning "to measure." Why do you think this name was chosen for this invention?

____

____

____

2. Imagine you are an explorer setting out across the ocean with just a compass to guide you. Write three sentences about how you feel.

____

____

____

3. Scientist Albert Einstein was fascinated by magnetism, the force that pulls compass needles. Einstein once said, "Anyone who has never made a mistake has never tried anything new." What do you think this means?

____

____

____

4. Compasses allowed people to explore the world. List some of the ways you think this changed people and their cultures.

____

____

____

5. Ancient people used early compasses to tell fortunes. How accurate do you think these predictions were? Explain your thinking.

____

____

____

Comets

What Are Comets?

Comets are space rocks in our solar system. People sometimes confuse comets with asteroids and meteoroids. It is important to know the difference between these space rocks.

Comets are small, irregularly shaped space rocks that are left over from the formation of the solar system. They are made of dust and ice, like a dirty snowball. They are often 1 to 10 kilometres across but can be up to 100 kilometres. Comets orbit the Sun. Many comets' orbits take them very close to the Sun. When they pass the Sun, they form a bright tail that can be seen from Earth.

Asteroids are space rocks that also orbit the Sun. Like comets, they are left over from the formation of the solar system. Asteroids are made mostly of rock and metals. Asteroids range in size from less than one kilometre across to hundreds of kilometres across. Unlike comets, asteroids never have a tail.

Meteoroids are small and rocky. They are formed when asteroids break up into smaller pieces or from dust given off by comets. They can be as small as a speck of dust or up to 10 metres across. They also orbit Earth. Sometimes meteoroids will fall into Earth's atmosphere and burn up. When they do, they can be seen in the sky, and we call them **meteors** or shooting stars. If a meteor does not burn up completely and hits Earth, we call it a **meteorite.**

Where Do Comets Come From?

Scientists believe that comets come from two areas in the solar system: the Kuiper Belt and the Oort Cloud. The Kuiper Belt begins just past Neptune's orbit around the Sun. It is a flat disk in the same position as the planets. The Oort Cloud is much farther away, at the very edge of our solar system. It is called a cloud because it surrounds the solar system completely.

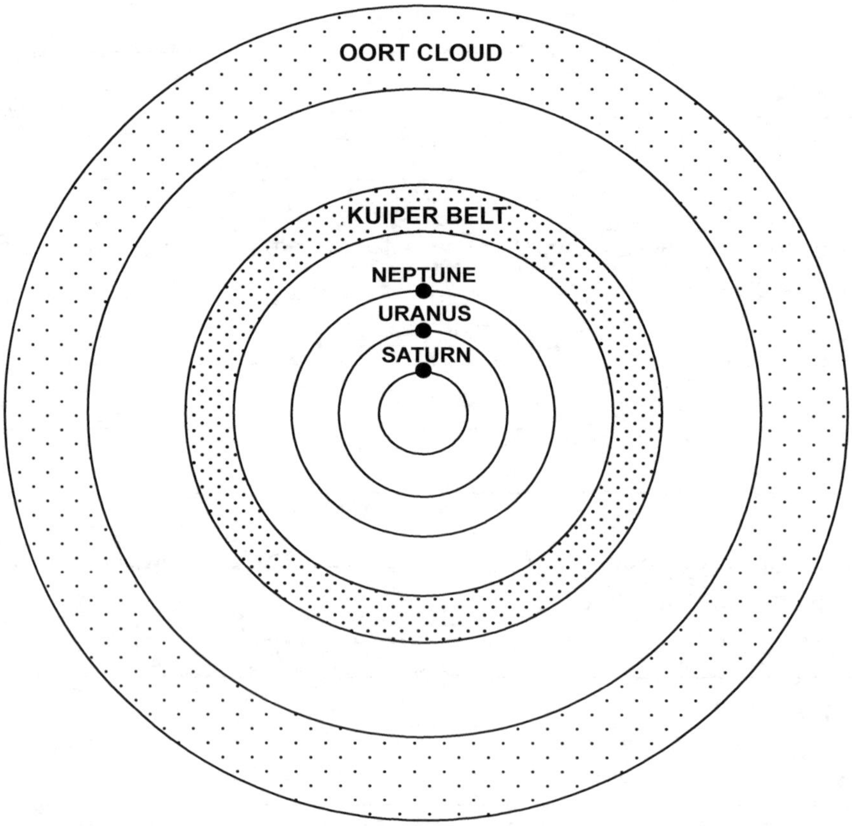

This diagram shows the positions of the last three planets, the Kuiper Belt, and the Oort Cloud. The Oort Cloud is like a huge ball around the solar system, even though it appears flat in this diagram.

Why Do We See Comets?

Scientists believe that the orbit, or path, of comets from the Kuiper Belt can change when they come close to the outer planets. This pulls them into the solar system. Comets from the Oort Cloud can also be pulled into the solar system but their orbit is changed by passing stars. The new orbits of these comets are elliptical, or oval shaped. The Sun is at one end of the oval.

We can see these comets when they are close to the Sun. This is because comets reflect the light from the Sun, just as our moon does. Also, the Sun melts the ice of a comet. This causes gases and dust to flow away, forming the comet's tail. A comet's tail can be thousands of kilometres long. This is when we can see a comet—when it is moving toward the Sun and when it is moving away from the Sun. Most of these comets cannot be seen with a telescope, but there are some spectacular comets that people can see just by looking at the sky. Unfortunately, these do not pass by very often.

What is wonderful about comets is that when you can see one, you can see it for a long time. It does not just whiz through the sky like a meteor.

Meteor Showers

Meteors appear as fast-moving streaks of light. During a meteor shower, you might see 40 or more streaks of light every hour in the same part of the night sky. Meteor showers can happen when Earth passes through the orbit of a comet. The comet is not there, but it has left behind dust or particles (meteoroids). As Earth passes through that cloud of meteoroids, many of the meteoroids fall into the atmosphere and light up the sky.

What Are Some Famous Comets?

Comets that come from the Kuiper Belt are short-period comets. This means that they complete one orbit in less than 200 years. Long-period comets come from the Oort Cloud. Their orbits are longer than 200 years.

Halley's comet is a short-period comet. It appears about every 75 years. The last time people could see it was in 1986. Spacecraft were sent up to take a closer look at the comet.

Hale-Bopp is a long-period comet. It is the most famous comet of recent times. Hale-Bopp was discovered in 1995. The comet's orbit brought it closest to Earth in 1997. Hale-Bopp was unusually bright, and could be seen with the naked eye in some parts of the world for about 18 months. Scientists predict Hale-Bopp will not return for thousands of years.

You can check the Internet for some great photographs of both of these famous comets.

"Comets"—Think About It

1. a) How are comets, asteroids, and meteoroids the same?

b) How is a comet different from an asteroid and a meteoroid?

c) How is an asteroid different from a comet and a meteoroid?

d) How is a meteoroid different from a comet and an asteroid?

2. Create a graphic organizer to show your answers to question 1.

"Comets"—Think About It (continued)

3. How are the Kuiper Belt and the Oort Cloud the same? How are they different?

4. Where did Halley's comet come from? Where did Hale-Bopp come from?

5. What is the same about all the subheadings in the text? How do they help you as a reader?

6. Is all the information in the text true? How do you know?

7. What does this text make you wonder about?

It Came from Space

Space exploration is very new in the history of humankind. Space travel began in 1957, when the first artificial satellite was launched by the Soviet Union. Yuri Gagarin became the first person to orbit Earth in 1961. In 1962, Alan Shepard became the first American to do the same thing. In 1969, Neil Armstrong became the first person to walk on the Moon.

Since then, space exploration has advanced very rapidly, and it has produced a large amount of amazing technology that we take for granted today. Technologies originally developed for use in space have found new and sometimes unexpected uses on Earth, in products called spin-offs. Here are just a few of the products we owe to space exploration.

Invisible Braces: A new material was developed to help track heat-seeking missiles. This new material is now used to make invisible braces.

Coatings for Lenses: A special coating was developed to protect plastic space equipment, such as visors for astronauts. This coating is used today to make plastic lenses that are very hard to scratch.

Smoke Detectors: Smoke detectors like the ones you use in your home were developed to detect fire or gases in *Skylab*, the first space station.

Cordless Tools: Lightweight, cordless tools were developed to help astronauts collect mineral and rock samples from the Moon.

CAT and MRI Scans: A technology was developed to photograph the Moon's surface and find a good place to land. CAT and MRI technologies were developed from this. They are used today in hospitals all around the world to produce images of the insides of people's bodies.

Memory Foam: A special foam was developed to protect astronauts from impact when landing. This foam is now used in many places such as airline seats, pillows, mattresses, and cushions for wheelchairs.

Blood Analysis Machine: Technology was developed to create a compact lab instrument that analyzes blood in 30 seconds rather than 20 minutes. This is used by doctors and hospitals today.

All of these technologies and many more help make our lives better.

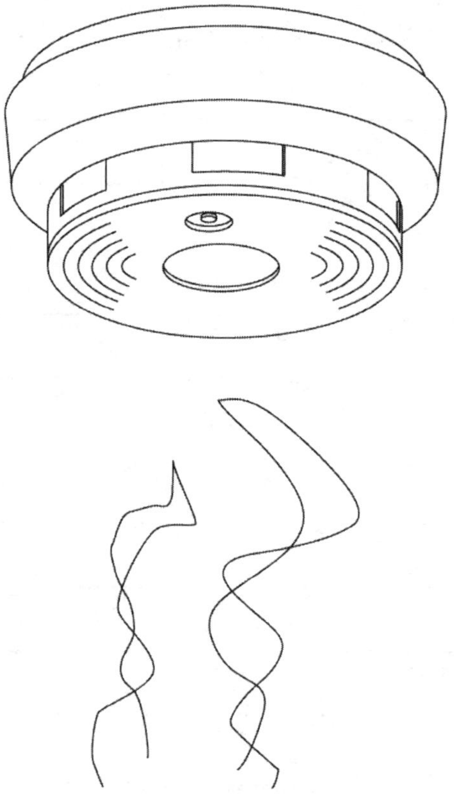

A smoke detector

"It Came from Space"—Think About It

1. Why does the author say that space exploration is new in the history of humankind?

2. When or why might it be important to do a blood analysis in 30 seconds?

3. What do you think the word *spin-off* means as used in this text? Why is this a good word for the technologies discussed in the text?

4. The Moon is a satellite that orbits (goes around) Earth. What do you think an *artificial satellite* is?

5. What is the central idea of this text? How does the author support the central idea?

6. How does the author feel about these technologies? Use specific details from the text to support your answer.

Scientific Classification

Organisms are living things. They range from the tallest trees to the tiniest bacteria. They live everywhere in the world, from the hot deserts to the cold oceans. Scientists classify organisms according to their similarities and differences. By using the same classification system, they can share their knowledge about organisms.

This system groups organisms into large categories, then into smaller and smaller categories according to their characteristics. The biggest categories are called **kingdoms**. The kingdoms are animals, plants, fungi, protista, and monera. People know the animal and plant kingdoms because there are so many animals and plants around us that we can see. Some organisms in the fungi kingdom might be familiar because this is the kingdom that includes mushrooms. Most organisms in the protista and monera kingdom are so tiny that a microscope is needed to see them. An amoeba is from the protista kingdom. Bacteria belong to the monera kingdom.

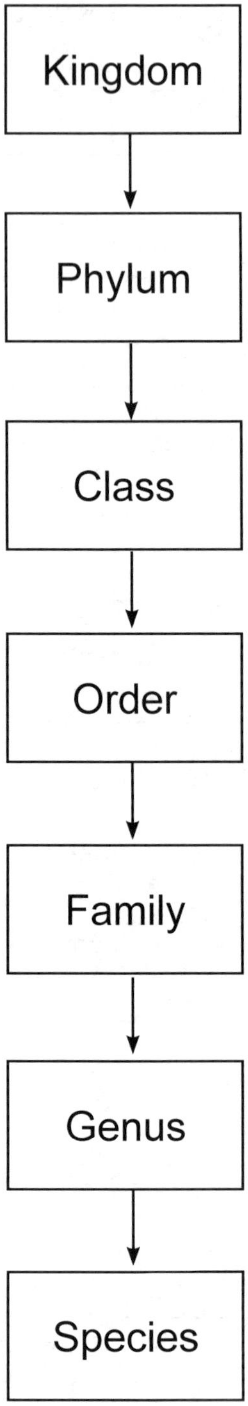

Kingdoms are the first of seven categories in the system. There are six more categories. Each category classifies organisms into smaller groups. As you move down the system, the organisms in each category become more and more like each other. So the categories from biggest to smallest are: kingdom, phylum, class, order, family, genus, and species. Let us see how this works by looking at domestic cats that we have as pets.

Kingdom The domestic cat belongs to the animal kingdom along with all the other animals in the world.

Phylum The cat belongs to the chordate phylum. This category includes all the animals that have backbones or spines.

Class The cat belongs to the mammal class. This category includes animals that give birth to live babies that the females feed with their own milk. Mammals also breathe through their lungs.

Order The cat belongs to the carnivore order. This category includes animals that eat other animals.

Family The cat belongs to the felidae family. This category includes all felids. (Felids are all the cats in the world, from lions and tigers to the domestic cat.)

Genus The cat belongs to the *felis* genus. This category includes all the wild and tame small cats in the world. Small cats do not roar.

Species All breeds of domestic cats belong to the species *catus*.

"Scientific Classification"—Think About It

1. Why might people not be familiar with organisms in the protista and monera kingdoms?

2. Which kingdom does a domestic cat belong to? Which phylum? Which class? Which order?

3. Scientists name organisms with two Latin names. The scientific name of the domestic cat is *felis catus*. Where do these names come from? How are these names like yours?

4. Why do you think it is important that scientists around the world use the same classification and naming system?

5. Think about how the classification system is organized. If you wanted to show how the system works using a geometric shape, such as a circle, which shape do you think would work best? Why?

6. How does the third paragraph relate to the list at the end?

Symbiosis

Symbiosis is a long-term relationship between two different species. This means that the two species interact with each other over a long period of time. So these types of relationships do not include things such as one species eating another one.

There are three main types of symbiosis. These are mutualism, commensalism, and parasitism. These may seem difficult to understand at first, but you probably already know many examples of these relationships.

Mutualism

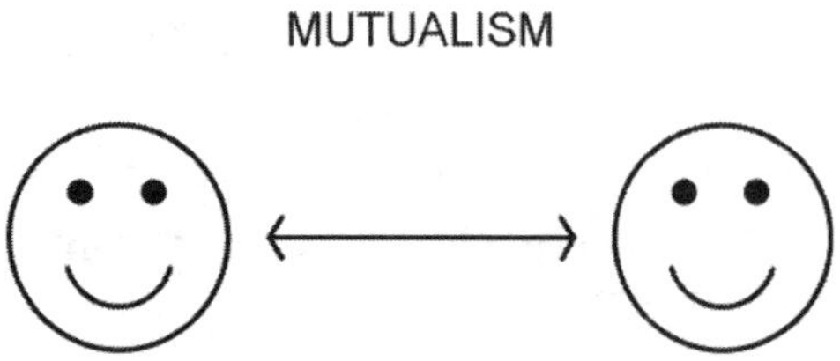

Mutualism comes from the word *mutual*, which means something that is shared by two or more organisms. In a mutual relationship, both organisms gain something. So you would have a mutual relationship with your best friend. Both of you benefit from the friendship. The same is true of mutualism in other species. In mutualism, both species have something to gain. Neither species is hurt by the relationship. There are many examples of this in the world. A honey bee collects pollen from flowers to make honey. While doing this, the bee pollinates the flower and helps it reproduce. The Plover bird cleans the teeth of a crocodile. The crocodile gets its teeth cleaned, and the bird gets something to eat. People even have symbiotic relationships with their pets. For example, a dog owner gives a dog food and shelter, and the dog gives the owner affection and companionship.

Commensalism

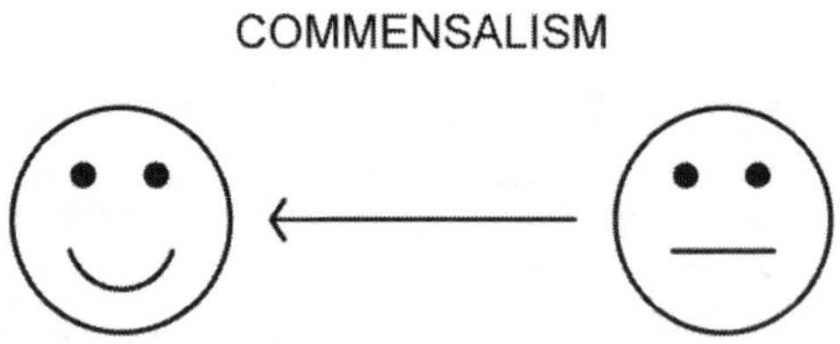

In commensalism, one species benefits from the relationship while the other species is not harmed. The Cattle egret, a type of bird, looks for food in fields where cattle live. The cattle stir up the ground as they move and eat the grass. This also brings insects to the surface. Egrets follow the cattle and eat the insects. So the egrets benefit by having their food "delivered," and the cattle are not harmed in any way. People have similar relationships with domestic animals. For example, people get eggs from chickens, and the chickens are not harmed.

Parasitism

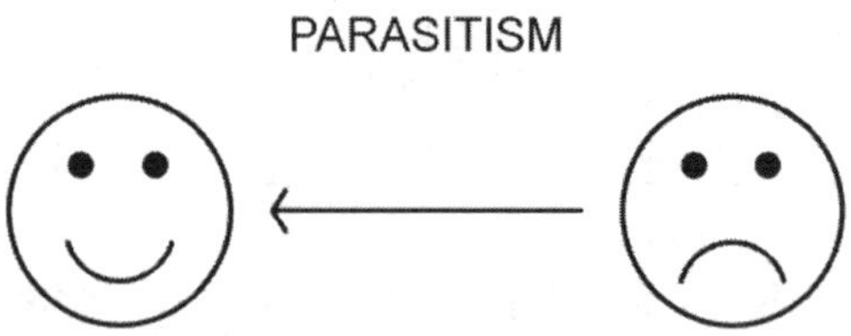

In biology, a parasite is an organism that lives on or in another organism (its host) and gets nourishment from it. In parasitism, the host is harmed in some way. One example is the tapeworm. A tapeworm gets inside the intestines of cows, pigs, and sometimes people. The tapeworm eats the host's partly digested food so the host does not get the nutrients it needs from the food. Another very common example is the mosquito. A mosquito bites its host to get blood to help its eggs develop. Mosquito bites can cause swelling and itching on the host. The bites can also spread diseases to their hosts.

"Symbiosis"—Think About It

1. Why is one animal eating another not an example of symbiosis?

2. Summarize this text in one paragraph.

3. How does the author introduce the idea of mutualism? How is this different from the way the author introduces the idea of commensalism?

4. Why is the word *delivered* in quotation marks in this sentence: So the egrets benefit by having their food "delivered"...?

5. Read the first sentence under Parasitism. Why do you think the author begins "In biology, a parasite is..."? What does this tell you about the word *parasite*?

6. How do the subheadings relate to the title of the text? How does the structure of the text help you as a reader?

Working Together

Most animals have a natural instinct to survive. (An instinct is a characteristic an animal is born with.) Some animals learn behaviours that will help them survive. All animals need to find food, stay alive in their environment, protect themselves from enemies, and reproduce to survive. Each animal has special characteristics or adaptations to help it survive. Some adaptations are physical—structures on or in the animals' bodies, such as beaks or colour. Some adaptations are behavioural—things animals do to survive, such as hibernating.

Some animals live in groups and cooperate with the other animals in the group to survive. Common examples of group cooperation are insects that live in colonies, such as bees and ants. All the individuals in these colonies work together for the survival of the colony.

Leaf-Cutter Ants

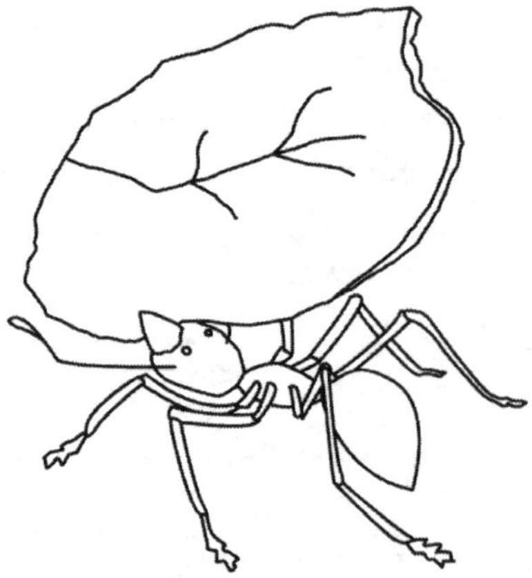

Leaf-cutter ants are very interesting. The larger ants go out to look for leaves. They bite off bits of leaves and carry them back to the nest. Watching these ants march in a single file, carrying bits of leaves, is quite a sight. These ants can carry a leaf that weighs 20 times more than they do. These larger ants are also responsible for defending the colony from predators.

The leaves the ants collect are not for eating. They are brought back to the colony and tucked away so fungus can grow on them. It is the fungus that is the food for the ants. This fungus is very unusual. It cannot survive outside the colony, and it cannot reproduce without the ants' help. Smaller ants in the colony grow the fungus on the leaves. They also look after the eggs that the queen ant lays.

Meerkats

Meerkats are another animal that lives in a cooperative group. A meerkat group is called a mob or gang. Meerkats live in underground tunnels and work together to help each other survive in their difficult environment. Meerkats share tasks such as watching their young, looking for enemies (particularly in the sky), and hunting for food. Meerkats are good hunters. When they are hunting smaller animals, they communicate with each other by making purring sounds.

Meerkats share their jobs, unlike leaf-cutter ants that each do only one job. But meerkats and leaf-cutter ants both work together in groups for the survival of all group members.

"Working Together"—Think About It

1. What are two types of adaptations that help animals survive? Explain and give an example of each.

2. What type of adaptation is living in groups?

3. What is unusual about the fungus that leaf-cutter ants eat? Use specific details from the text to support your answer.

4. The word *common* has many meanings. Find the sentence in the text that has this word. Which one of these synonyms of common is closest to the meaning of the word in the text: *ordinary, familiar, normal, shared, rough*?

5. What is the main idea of the text? Where is the main idea introduced? How does the author develop this main idea?

6. What is the first paragraph about? Why do you think the author started with this paragraph?

Autumn Days

When summer is over, cool winds begin to blow. The season of autumn, or fall, brings many changes to plants, animals, and people.

Colour-Changing Trees

As summer comes to an end, the days begin to get shorter and cooler. That gives trees the signal that winter is coming. Throughout the spring and summer, a substance in the leaves called chlorophyll (you say it like this: *KLOHR-uh-fill*) helps the trees manufacture food. Chlorophyll also makes leaves green. By the time autumn is here, leaves stop making food and the chlorophyll disappears. The yellows and oranges that are hidden in the leaves are now visible. Some leaves are red because they contain a sugar called glucose (you say it like this: *GLOO-cohs*).

All across Canada, trees such as maples, oaks, and birches begin to turn gold, orange, and red. These trees are called deciduous (you say it like this: *duh-SID-yoo-uss*) trees and they lose their leaves in autumn. But some trees stay green and do not lose their leaves, even throughout the winter. These are coniferous (you say it like this: *KON-iff-fer-uss*) trees, such as pines, spruces, and firs.

A Colour-Changing Bird

Many birds fly south in autumn when temperatures begin to drop. Robins, waxwings, bluebirds, and other birds migrate to warmer places when cold winds begin to blow. But some birds are able to stay warm and find enough to eat, even when snow covers the ground. Blue jays, cardinals, and chickadees all brighten grey winter days. They eat food people put out in bird feeders, as well as seeds and berries they can find in gardens and fields.

In the Arctic, the ptarmigan (you say it like this: *TAR-mih-gun*) stays in the north all year round, but it changes colour in the autumn. During the summer, this bird is mostly brown. As winter approaches, its brown feathers are replaced with off-white feathers. They make the ptarmigan difficult to see against the winter snow.

A Long Nap

Some animals survive the winter by sleeping throughout the long, cold months. This deep sleep is called hibernation. In autumn, hibernating animals begin to eat a lot. They need to put on lots of fat to give them the energy they will need while they are sleeping. These animals hibernate because the foods they eat are very hard to find during the winter.

Animals such as groundhogs, snakes, and bats all hibernate. They find a safe cave, or burrow, where they can rest. When they are hibernating, their body temperature drops very low and they breathe very slowly. They do not eat and they are hard to wake up.

Most people think bears hibernate but they do not. They sleep a lot during winter, but they wake up easily. As well, their breathing speed decreases only a little.

"Autumn Days"—Think About It

1. What are three details that support the subheading Colour-Changing Trees?

2. What is the difference between deciduous trees and coniferous trees? Give two examples of each.

3. How does the ptarmigan prepare for winter? Explain why.

4. What changes do you notice in the fall where you live?

5. Why do hibernating animals begin to eat a lot in the autumn?

6. How does hibernation benefit some animals? Use details from the text and your own ideas.

Stick It

Have you ever rubbed a balloon with a piece of wool, then put it on a wall? What happens? The balloon sticks to the wall. You probably know that the balloon sticks because of static electricity. But do you know how static electricity works?

The Atom

To understand static electricity, you need to know about the atom. Atoms make up matter. Matter includes everything in our world, from the air we breathe to the food we eat. Even our bodies are matter. Matter is anything that takes up space and has mass. (Mass is how much of something there is.) If you could take a look inside an atom, you would see three things: protons, electrons, and neutrons. The protons and neutrons make up the nucleus of the atom. The electrons move around outside the nucleus.

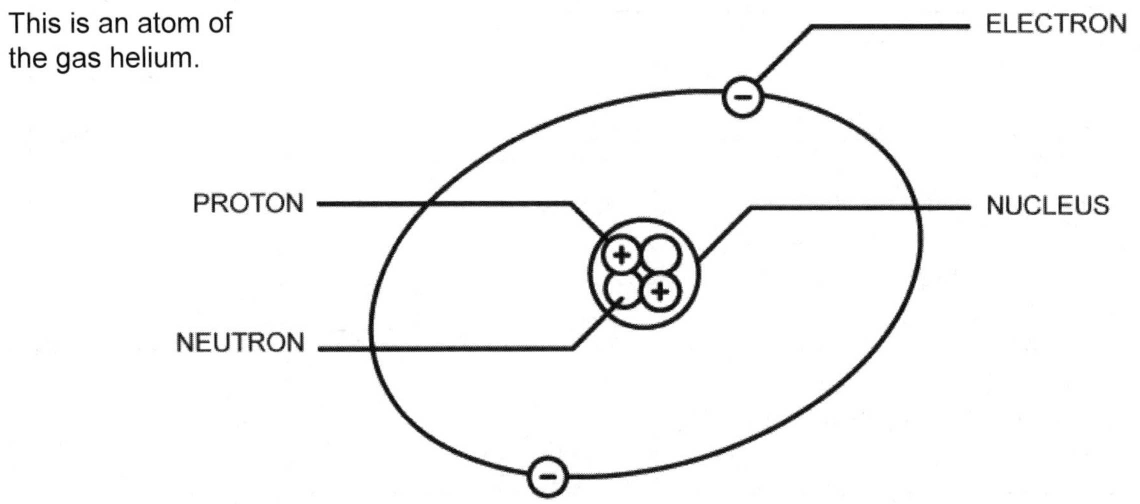

You can see that an electron has a minus sign and a proton has a plus sign. This is because the electron has a negative electrical charge. The proton has a positive electrical charge. The neutron has no charge. When an atom has an equal number of protons and electrons, it has an equal number of positive and negative charges, so the charge of the entire atom is neutral. We can also say that the atom has no charge. So most matter has no electrical charge. This means most things in our world are neutral when it comes to electricity. But this can change.

Static Electricity

Static electricity happens when negative charges (electrons) are moved from one object to another. When you rub the balloon with the wool, you move electrons from the wool to the balloon. So now the wool has more protons and fewer electrons and has a positive charge. The balloon picks up these electrons, so now it has more electrons than protons and has a negative charge. You have created static electricity. The negatively charged balloon is attracted to positively charged areas of the wall. But the balloon does not stick to the wall for very long. Soon, the extra electrons on the balloon go into the air and the balloon is neutral again. It is no longer attracted to the wall.

"Stick It"—Think About It

1. Write a sentence describing a negatively charged object. Write a sentence describing a positively charged object.

____

____

2. How could you make a balloon stick to a wall longer? Why would this work?

____

____

____

3. In science, something is *neutral* if it does not have a positive or negative charge. What object in the text has a name similar to *neutral?* Why do you think it was given that name?

____

____

____

4. Why did the author describe atoms before explaining static electricity?

____

____

____

5. Draw a diagram to show what happens to electrons when a balloon is rubbed with a piece of wool. Did drawing the diagram help you as a reader? Why or why not?

____

____

6. Does the diagram of the atom give you any more information than was in the text? Why do you think the author included the diagram?

____

____

____

Graphic Organizers

Graphic organizers are excellent tools to use for identifying and organizing information from a text into an easy-to-understand visual format. Students will expand their comprehension of a text as they complete the graphic organizers. Use these graphic organizers in addition to the activities in this book or with other texts.

Concept Web – Helps students understand the main idea of a text and how it is supported by key details.

Concept Map – Helps students gain a better understanding of how different subtopics within a text connect to the topic as a whole.

Venn Diagram/Comparison Chart – Helps students focus on the comparison of two items, such as individuals, ideas, events, or pieces of information. Students could compare by looking at which things are the same, or contrast by looking at which things are different.

Fact or Opinion – Helps students to distinguish between statements of fact or opinion. Facts are pieces of information that can be proven to be true. Opinions are pieces of information based on something that someone thinks or believes, but that cannot necessarily be proven to be true.

Cause and Effect – Helps students to recognize and explain relationships between events. The cause is the reason why an event happens and the effect is the event that happens.

Making Connections – Helps students to connect something they have read, or experienced, with the world around them.

Context Clue Chart – Helps students organize clues that the author gives in a text to help define a difficult or unusual word. Encourage students to look for explanations of words within a text.

Drawing Conclusions and Making Inferences Chart – Helps students practice drawing conclusions and making inferences based on their prior knowledge, as well as what they read in the text.

A Concept Web About...

A **main idea** is what the text is mostly about. A **detail** is important information that tells more about the main idea.

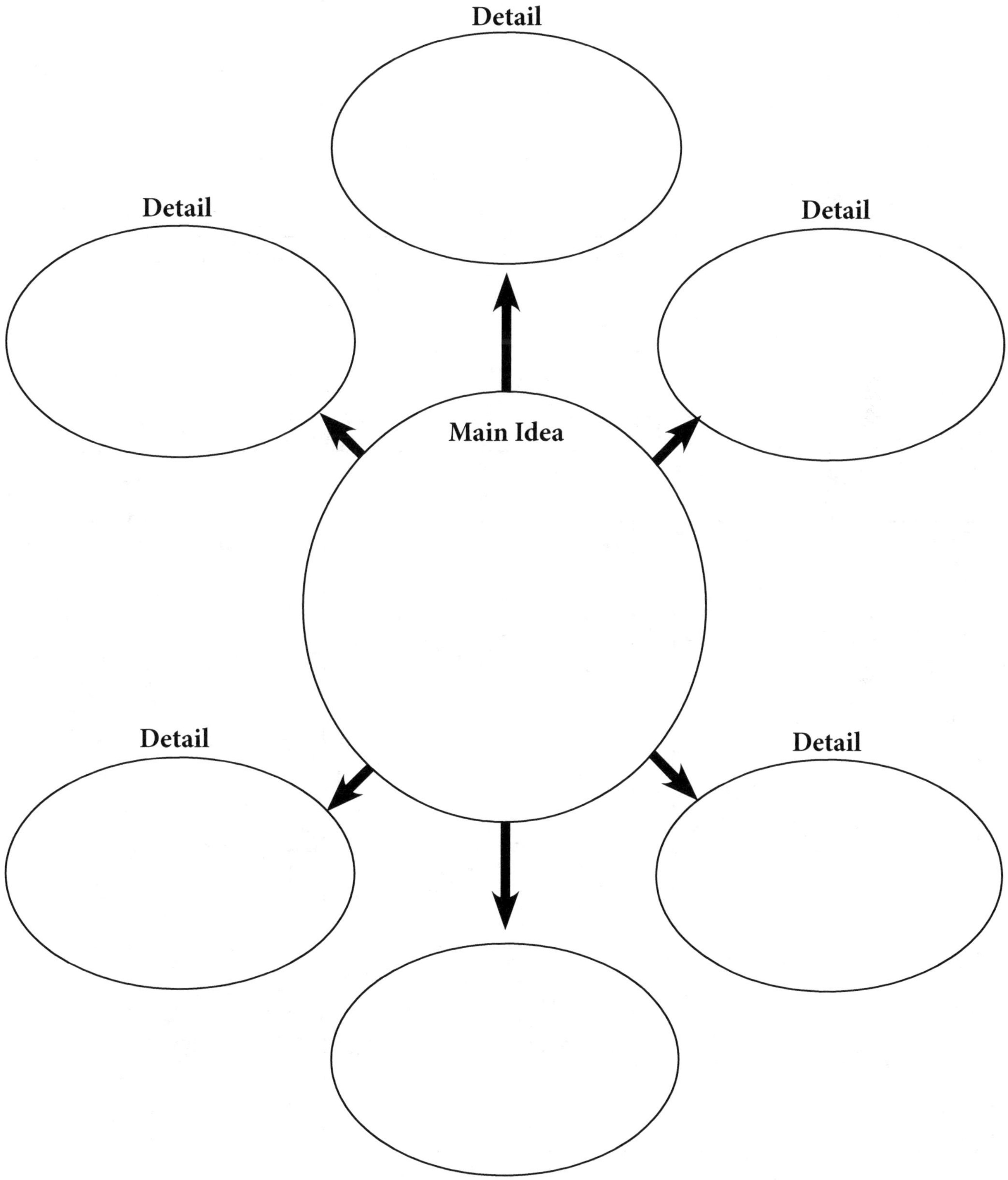

Concept Map

A **main idea** is what the text is mostly about.
A **subheading** is the title given to a part of a text.
A **detail** is important information that tells more about the main idea.

Main Idea

Subheading

Subheading

Subheading

Details

Details

Details

A Venn Diagram About...

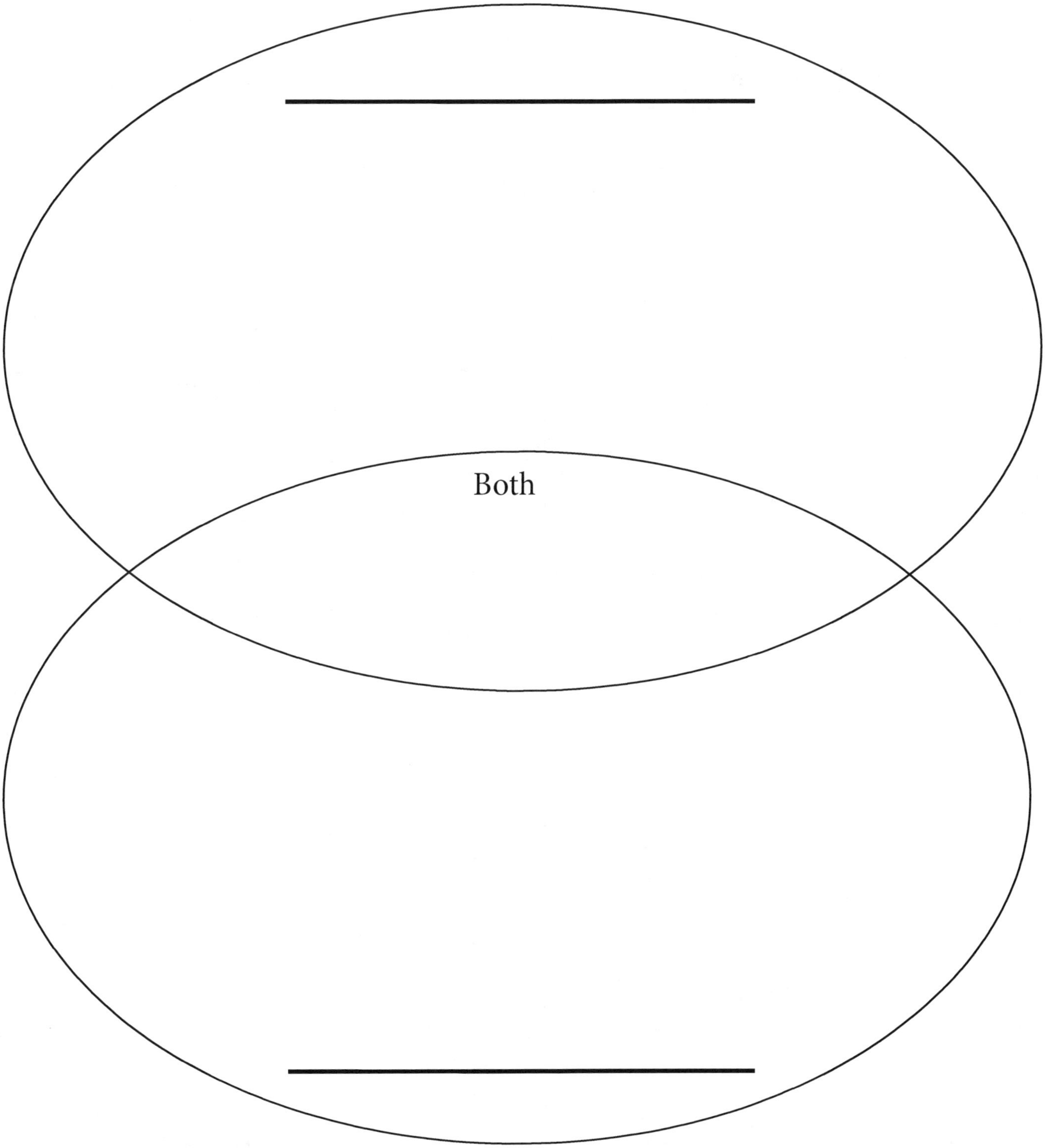

A Comparison Chart

Compared to

Detailed information

Detailed information

Fact or Opinion

- **Facts** are pieces of information that can be proven to be true.
- **Opinions** are pieces of information based on something a person thinks or believes.

Piece of Information	Fact or Opinion?	How do you know?

Cause and Effect

- The **cause** is the reason something happens.
- The **effect** is what happened.

Cause **Effect**

Making Connections with What I Have Read

After reading...	It reminds me of...	This helps me make a connection to...
		☐ something else I have read ☐ myself ☐ the world around me
		☐ something else I have read ☐ myself ☐ the world around me
		☐ something else I have read ☐ myself ☐ the world around me
		☐ something else I have read ☐ myself ☐ the world around me

Context Clue Chart

Context Clues are hints that the author gives in a text that can help you find the meaning of a word.

Word	Context Clue from Text	Meaning of Word

Drawing Conclusions and Making Inferences Chart

We make an **inference** when we combine what we know to be true with new information and come to a conclusion.

What I already know:	Clues from the text I read:	What I can conclude or infer:

How Am I Doing?

	Completing my work	Using my time wisely	Following directions	Keeping organized
Full speed ahead!	• My work is always complete and done with care. • I added extra details to my work.	• I always get my work done on time.	• I always follow directions.	• My materials are always neatly organized. • I am always prepared and ready to learn.
Keep going!	• My work is complete and done with care. • I added extra details to my work.	• I usually get my work done on time.	• I usually follow directions without reminders.	• I usually can find my materials. • I am usually prepared and ready to learn.
Slow down!	• My work is complete. • I need to check my work.	• I sometimes get my work done on time.	• I sometimes need reminders to follow directions.	• I sometimes need time to find my materials. • I am sometimes prepared and ready to learn.
Stop!	• My work is not complete. • I need to check my work.	• I rarely get my work done on time.	• I need reminders to follow directions.	• I need to organize my materials. • I am rarely prepared and ready to learn.

Reading Comprehension Student Tracking Sheet

Student's Name	**Identifies the Purpose of the Text** *Student: I can tell you why we read this.*	**Demonstrates Understanding of the Text** *Student: I can tell you what the text is about.*	**Analyzes Text** *Student: I can make predictions, interpretations, and conclusions using information from the text.*	**Makes Connections to Text (Prior Knowledge)** *Student: This reminds me of* • *text-to-text* • *text-to-self* • *text-to-world*	**Text Features** *Student: I can tell you how different text features help the reader.*

Level 4: Student shows a thorough understanding of all or almost all concepts and consistently gives appropriate and complete explanations independently. No teacher support is needed.
Level 3: Student shows a good understanding of most concepts and usually gives complete or nearly complete explanations. Infrequent teacher support is needed.
Level 2: Student shows a satisfactory understanding of most concepts and sometimes gives appropriate but incomplete explanations. Teacher support is sometimes needed.
Level 1: Student shows little understanding of concepts and rarely gives complete explanations. Intensive teacher support is needed.

Achievement Certificate

You Are Doing Well!

Keep Up the Excellent Work!

Name

Date

Reading Comprehension

Answers

How to Be a Good Babysitter, pp. 4–5

1. Think about being a helper in a home while the parents are there, talk to other people who do babysit, and read about babysitting on the Internet and in books.
2. If you did not know about allergies, you might feed a child something that would make him or her very sick. If you did not know what a child was afraid of, you might do or say something that would make him or her afraid.
3. In a list explaining how to do or make something, the ideas would be in the order they need to be done. The order is important. In this text, the order is not important. The points in the list could be written in any order.
4. The author's point of view is that babysitting is a great responsibility and it is important to know how to do the job well. The author gives tips on how to do the job well. In the tips, the author talks about responsibilities and how important they are.
5. The author means that keeping another person safe, healthy, and happy is a big job. It is a great responsibility. Maybe not everyone is ready to do all those things.
6. The text is opinion. It is the author's ideas about babysitting and how to be a good babysitter. Some people might not agree with some of the author's ideas. There are no facts that are true and that everyone would agree on.

Build Up That Body, pp. 6–7

1. When your muscles push and pull against your bones, it helps make your bones stronger.
2. When you do cardiovascular activities, your heart pumps faster. Anything that makes your heart beat fster and gets you breathing faster will help your heart improve.
3. If you are flexible you can do things such as stretching to reach something or bending down to pick up something. You can move your body in different ways easily. You can do exercises or activities more easily. If you were not very flexible, you could not do many things easily. You might hurt yourself by stretching or bending.
4. Some activities are best for improving different components. Push-ups will help muscle strength. Tennis will help muscle endurance. Gymnastics will help flexibility. Swimming will help cardiovascular fitness. Some activities such as running will help more than one component of physical fitness.
5. Cardiovascular fitness uses these terms. Cardiovascular fitness is about how well your heart pumps blood and oxygen through blood vessels to all parts of the body.
6. The main idea is that being physically fit is good for you. The author expands on this by explaining four components of physical fitness and how each of these helps your body.

Do It Safely, pp. 8–9

1. Do different activities, get exercise regularly, and do activities that you enjoy to get the most out of physical activity.
2. You should warm up before doing an activity so your muscles can get moving before you work them hard. You would not need to warm up for an easy walk because the walk is like warming up. You would not be working your muscles hard in an easy walk.
3. You should stop so you do not hurt yourself more. If you do not stop, the injury might get worse.
4. Choose the right equipment for the activity you are doing. Equipment can be helmets, goggles, face guards, mouth guards, and footwear. Warm up before doing exercise or an activity to give your muscles a chance to get moving. Do not do an activity if you hurt yourself or are sick. Wait until you are better. Follow the rules because they will protect you.
5. Wearing the right equipment will help keep you safe when you do an activity or play a sport. When you ride a bicycle, wear a bicycle helmet.

Treating Minor Injuries, pp. 10–11

1. A strain is when a muscle is stretched too far or tears. A sprain is when a ligament stretches or tears. I think a sprain is more serious because a sprain could be a bone fracture.
2. If the bandage is too tight, it might stop blood flowing.
3. You can treat minor injuries by yourself, but if the injury is serious, you should go to a doctor.
4. The words are protect, rest, ice, compress, and elevate. I know because these words have bold letters in the list that explains what PRICE is.
5. It means that it is better to do something than be sorry after that you did not do it. In this text it means that it is better to go to a doctor for an injury rather than hurting yourself more and being sorry that you did not see a doctor.
6. Each description tells how to treat the injury and when you should go to a doctor because of the injury. This information could have been presented in a two-column chart with one column telling how to treat the injury and the second telling when to go to a doctor.

Blog or News? pp. 12–13

1. The first item includes facts that can bechecked and does not include the author's opinion.
2. The news article is all facts about the book, the author, the main character, and about the first book. The blog has some facts too, such as the names of the two books, the author, and the main character. The writing in the news article is more formal. The writing in the blog is informal. You do not know who wrote the news article, but the name of the writer of the blog is given. The blog gives the writer's opinion of the book. He wants people to read the book. The news article does not give an opinion. It just gives information on buying the book.
3. Formal writing sounds like writing you would find in a newspaper or a school book. Informal writing sounds as though you are talking to a friend.
4. I would write a news article so people would know the facts about the play, such as what it is, when it will be performed, how much a ticket costs. OR I would write a blog telling how great I think the play is to get people excited about coming. I could put facts about the play in the blog too. OR I would write both because that way I could give all the information they would need about the play, and I could give my opinion about it too.
5. The main idea is that there is a difference between a news article and a blog. The author supports this by giving an example of a news article and a blog about the same topic. This helps me understand the differences better.
6. Sequel means something that comes after something else. *The Far Away Country* is a sequel to the first book so it is a book that comes after the first book.

How *Star Wars* Changed Moviemaking Forever, pp. 14–16

1. Answers will vary.
2. Many new special effects were created for *Star Wars*, and the company that created them continues to work on movies today. *Star Wars* was so popular, it set box office records and made a lot of money for movie-theatre owners. Owners built more screens and theatres, including the multiplexes we have today, and more people made different types of movies to show on all the new screens.
3. Inventors have even tried to create some of the things you see in the movies, including the hologram images and the huge AT-AT robots.
4. The director is George Lucas.
5. R2-D2 and C-3PO are robots from *Star Wars*. ASIMO and REEM-A are real-life robots.
6. Movie robots are smarter than real-life robots and can do many things. For example, C-3PO looked and behaved like a human and was programmed to speak many languages.

Camera Language, pp. 17–18

1. I could use a video recorder, a digital camera, or a smart phone. I could edit my video using programs on the Internet. I could show my video on my television or my computer.
2. In the list, the names of the shots are in bold. This could help me find the shots I want more quickly. I just have to look at the bold words.
3. They are arranged in order from beginning to end.
4. I would use a high camera shot if I wanted to show that the subject was weak. I would use a low camera shot when I wanted to make the subject look powerful.
5. The author described what a storyboard is because that is where you would use camera language first. The author is giving you a purpose for knowing camera language.
6. I think the fade-in, fade-out, and dissolve would be done when editing because cameras cannot do those things. You would need to add them into the video. All the others could be done with a camera.

Phones on the Go, pp. 19–21

1. Martin Cooper may have first called his rival to let the man know Cooper had succeeded in inventing the cell phone. He may have wanted to make sure his rival was up to date with his latest news or he may have wanted to gloat!
2. Answers will vary. Ensure that students provide reasons for their point of view.
3. "No one would look twice" means that no one would think the action is abnormal. The author used this phrase to illustrate how common cell phones have become.
4. Answers will vary. Ensure students provide reasons for their point of view.
5. Answers will vary.
6. The subheadings tell me what each section is about before I read it. The information could be set up in a two-column table, with the headings in the first column and the information in the second column.

The Computer Revolution, pp. 22–24

1. Early computers were huge because they were powered by many large vacuum tubes. Computers today are powered by transistors. Transistors are tiny and getting smaller.
2. Smaller computers allow people to carry them around or have more than one in their home. In offices, the computers take up less valuable working space. It also makes it possible to pack more computers into less space, making more computing power easily available.
3. Answers will vary. Sample answers: How Computers Have Changed, Computers Through the Years, Computer Evolution
4. a) In addition to using computers to communicate, for research, and for entertainment, students may have used many other computers without realizing it. Computers run refrigerators, toasters, cars, buses, stop lights, and many more devices.
   b) Answers will vary.

Cool As a Cucumber, pp. 25–27

1. A good, useful expression involves things, such as fruit, that everyone is familiar with. That makes the expression easy to understand. A good expression is also easy to remember—it rhymes or has interesting wordplay. A useful expression is also about situations that people often encounter.
2. Eat an apple on going to bed, and you'll keep the doctor from earning his bread.
3. Some people think the expression comes from the Persian or Hindi word *chiz*, which means "thing."
4. Possible answers: to pass along advice, to help other people, to show how smart they are, to share their experience.
5. Old televisions had tubes in them and potatoes are a type of tuber. The sentence in the text that tells me this is "Old televisions had tubes inside them and potatoes are a type of plant known as a tuber, so that is how the two became connected."
6. Sample answer: "You cannot make an omelette without breaking eggs." This expression means that you cannot make something good (such as a tasty omelette) without first making a bit of a mess. The eggs get messy when you break them, but they turn into something nice and tasty when they become an omelette.

Science Fiction and Fantasy, pp. 28–29

1. *Ender's Game* takes place in the future. There is special technology in the story. There are aliens from another planet. Ender is in a situation that a young boy could not be in today. *The Neverending Story* takes place in this world and in a fantasy world. The young boy goes on a journey to find the ruler of the country. He meets dragons, giants, and other monsters.
2. The setting of a fantasy story can be in a fantasy world. The story can start in the real world and sometimes the whole story is set in a fantasy world. Sometimes the story starts in the real world but moves to a fantasy world. Sometimes the setting can be the real world but magical and supernatural things happen.
3. The science should fit with something that is happening today or be something that scientists hope they will be able to do in the future.
4. The two main topics are science fiction and fantasy novels. The author explains what each of these are by giving characteristics of each one. Then the author gives an example of a novel for each and tells a little about the novels.
5. The author gives the definition in a separate part of the text. The definition is not part of the text. The author could have put the definition in the text in the first paragraph. I like having the definition separate because knowing what the definition is first helps me understand the information better. OR I like having everything in the text so I do not have to go back and forth when I am reading.

6. I think *mock* means something that is not real because Ender is training for war. This means that he would not be fighting in real battles but pretend ones.

Harry and Katniss, pp. 30–31

1. It means that you do not know what is happening. You do not know about popular things. The author says that Harry and Katniss are characters in two of the most popular series today. So if you do not know who they are, you do not know or do not care about things that are popular.
2. You could put subheadings before the third paragraph and before the fourth paragraph. The first subheading could be Timelines of Series Books. The second subheading could be Why Readers Like Series Books.
3. This is a book in a series that can be read at any time. It does not matter where in the series the book comes. This is because what happened before in the series is not important.
4. The author says that the books have sold over 100 million copies and have been made into successful movies. I think the claim is true because you could check to find out how many books were sold and if the movies were successful.
5. Readers like the main characters and want to know what happens to them. Readers want to find out what happens at the end of the series so they keep reading the books.
6. They are the same because each book has to have an ending for that book. They are different because the ending of a book in a series must also link to the next book in the series.

The Magic Mirror, pp. 32–34

1. The women were afraid that they had faults (or were aware that they did) and would probably be embarrassed or ashamed if they looked in the mirror and dark spots appeared. (Students might also mention that women would fear being publicly embarrassed—the crowd outside the barber's shop would realize that a woman had failed the test if she did not later marry the king.)
2. A king usually wants to marry a woman who comes from a wealthy or noble family. Most kings would not marry a girl who worked tending sheep, even if she had no faults.
3. a) The barber probably thought that the story about the mirror would be a good way to encourage a woman of good character to come forward, and to discourage women who knew that they did not have good character.
   b) Students might suggest answers such as the following:
   - If a woman knew that she did not have good character and was brave enough to look in the mirror, no spots would have appeared and she might have married the king.
   - The king might have punished the barber if he found out the barber lied to him about the mirror being magic.
   - People might no longer trust the barber, since he lied about the mirror.
4. Students might suggest the following ideas:
   - The girl was confident enough to look into the mirror.
   - The girl was honest enough to admit that she sometimes made mistakes.
   - The girl was loving and protective of her sheep; being loving and protective are good qualities for a wife and future mother.

The Wise Chief and His Wife, pp. 35–37

1. The chief was happy because he liked using his wisdom to solve difficult problems, and because he liked impressing the villagers with his wisdom.
2. The chief did not want people to think there was anyone in the village as wise as he was.
3. a) Shamika gave one of the boys an answer because she knew the boy had told the truth.
   b) Possible answers include the following:
   - Shamika believes strongly in honesty and fairness. She helped the boy who told the truth because it was only fair that the boy who stole the sheep should have to return it.
   - Shamika is brave (or unselfish) because she knew that she was taking a risk in helping the boy, and she would have to return to her father's house if the chief found out.
   - Shamika believes that sometimes breaking a rule is the right thing to do.
4. Most students will likely believe that Shamika is wiser because she was able to figure out a way to make the chief forgive her and let her come back.

Body Language: What Does It Mean? pp. 38–39

1. The person might slump in a chair, tap fingers, or not look at a person talking.
2. Facial expressions do not change much from culture to culture. So someone who was surprised would have the same facial expression in Canada and in India.
3. *Nonverbal communication* is communicating with someone without using sound or words. *Verbal* means to communicate with sound and words. Verbal would be the opposite of nonverbal because the prefix *non* means "not."
4. The author claims that we can use body language as clues to better understand what a person is thinking or feeling. The author supports this by giving examples of body language and what it might mean. I think the claim is valid because I have seen people do what the author describes. AND/OR I sometimes use body language the way the author describes it.
5. Sample answer: If I wanted to make a good impression on someone, I would do things with my body to show that I am interested. I would look at the person, stand or sit up straight, smile, and not tap my fingers.
6. It means that body language cannot be proven the way things in other science can. It is not the same as knowing something to be true all the time. Sometimes body language will mean what they say it does but sometimes it will not.

Galileo and His Telescope, pp. 40–41

1. Galileo proved that Earth and the other planets orbit around the Sun. The church and government believed that Earth was the centre of everything in the universe. They made him say he was wrong.
2. When you looked at something through the telescope it looked 30 times bigger than it was.
3. Thermometers today tell us what the temperature is. Galileo's thermometer only showed if one temperature was higher, lower, or the same as another temperature.
4. Because you could see things that were far away, you would be able to look at people without them knowing. This is the same as spying.
5. Scientists test their ideas to see if they work. Galileo did this by looking at space through a telescope. He could see what things in space looked like and what they did. He did not believe what he had been told about what happened in space. He wanted proof.
6. Galileo built a telescope that let him look at things in space, such as the planet Jupiter. He invented things such as the first thermometer. He was a real scientist who tested his ideas.

Chris Hadfield, pp. 42–43

1. He was the first and only Canadian to board the *Mir* space station. He was the first Canadian to walk in space.
2. *Mission* means a trip in space. The word is used in the text when it tells about the trips Chris made.
3. NASA is the acronym. I know because I have heard the word before. You can put the letters together and they make a word. CSA and ISS are initialisms. You cannot pronounce the letters as a word.
4. I think the author likes and admires Chris. The author starts off by saying there is a lot more to Chris than his singing. Then the author lists all the important things Chris has done. The author does not write anything that is not good about Chris.
5. The dates tell when the different things in Chris's life happened.
6. The author might have wanted the reader to know what kind of person Chris Hadfield is. The quote tells me that he does take his job seriously but he still gets excited about it. I think he has a good sense of humour because the quote is funny.

Wayne Gretzky, pp. 44–45

1. He is famous for being a great hockey player.
2. He practised four or five hours a day with his brothers. It helped him become a good hockey player because you need to practise a lot at something to be good.
3. *Agile* means to be able to do things in sports with your body without stopping or falling down. The text says that Wayne could change direction and not lose his balance or slow down when he was skating. He could do this because he was agile.
4. Wayne would pass to his teammates if he thought they could score a goal.
5. The author thinks Wayne was a great hockey player. The author explains all the great things he could do on the ice. The author also explains how Wayne helped his teammates and how he played his best all the time. The author thinks Wayne is a nice person. The author explains the good things Wayne did for others.
6. The quotation is about trying. It means that if you do not try then you will not do anything. You need to try to be good at what you do.

In Flanders Fields, pp. 46–48

1. "In Flanders Fields" was such a successful poem because it captured how people were feeling at the time. It is not too long so people do not lose interest when reading it. It also sounds good when it is read out loud. There are powerful images in the poem and people can see the pictures clearly. The poem starts quietly, builds to a strong climax, and ends solidly.
2. Answers will vary. Ensure students include an explanation as to why they liked the line.
3. John McCrae was a doctor in charge of the medical station that was in the middle of the battles happening in Flanders.
4. John McCrae showed his courage by taking part in a number of wars. He was brave enough to work close to where the fighting was taking place and he kept on working even when he was in danger.
5. These lines encourage future soldiers to be brave and to continue to fight. Even though the dead soldiers have had to stop battling, they want the living soldiers to be strong and not give up.
6. A lark is a type of bird. I know this because the poem says that they sing and fly. Birds do these things

Camp X, pp. 49–50

1. Sample answer: It was important for Camp X to stay a secret because the enemy would have loved to destroy it. I know this because the text says "While the conflict raged in Europe, the camp was top secret, since enemy spies would have loved to destroy it."
2. Possible answer: I think the author mentioned that Stephenson only had a Grade 6 education because he or she wanted us to know how smart Stephenson was and how much he was able to do even though he did not finish school. I also think he or she wanted the reader to know that everyone is gifted in their own way and can be smart even if they do not go to school.
3. Answers will vary.
4. Words that can describe spies include clever, stealthy, deadly, bloodthirsty, confident, untrustworthy, close-mouthed, and quick-witted.
5. People think Intrepid was so important in World War II because he, and the spies he trained, figured out enemy code, forged documents, and sabotaged German experiments. Intrepid also set up a spy network, exposed German spies, and protected Allied factories in North America from sabotage.
6. Today Camp X is a park that anyone can visit, and there is a museum nearby. Spies do not train there anymore, and it is no longer a secret.

How Fire Changed the World, pp. 51–52

1. People used to sit around fires to stay warm and tell stories. Many people who sit around fires today do so for the same reasons. The difference between people then and people today is that people used to have to sit around fires because it was the only way to stay warm. Today we choose to sit around fires to stay warm and tell stories.
2. Wheels are used for moving people and things, including food. People paved roads after the wheel was invented because wheels move better on smooth roads. Those roads linked cities together, so society changed as people traded goods. Cars, trucks, and bicycles depend on wheels, and so do clocks, computers, and motors. Many potters need potter's wheels to make bowls, jugs, etc. The gyroscope, propeller, and turbine are all based on the wheel.
3. Answers will vary. Ensure that students write five sentences.
4. Cooked food is easier for the human body to process than raw food. Cooked food helped people to become taller and bigger. It also helped people to live longer.
5. Fire protected people from insects and wild animals because the animals were afraid of the heat and light. The insects were kept away by the smoke.
6. Fire can hurt or kill people. It can destroy homes and other buildings, as well as forests, grasslands, and other environments, and the animals that live there. People's belongings can also be destroyed by fire and so can irreplaceable works of art. The smoke from fires can harm and pollute the air and surroundings.

Horses in North America, pp. 53–54

1. No one knows for sure but horses might have disappeared because of disease or climate change.
2. Before the horses disappeared in North America, they crossed over to Siberia and spread through Europe and Asia. So it was the horses that came from those horses that were brought to North America.

3. *Introduce* is the root word. Introduce means to bring something to a new place to live. The prefix *re* means to do something again. *Reintroduce* means to bring something to a place to live where it had lived before.
4. They lived where there were birch trees. They lived where there were many steams and rivers.
5. Riding horses made it easier for them to hunt animals. They were migratory people so they could move themselves and their goods more easily by horse than on foot.
6. The map shows the reader where the Bering Land Bridge used to be that horses used to cross into Europe thousands of years ago.

The Women of the Haudenosaunee Confederacy, pp. 55–56

1. The Haudenosaunee Confederacy was formed by a group of nations so they could live in peace. So it was an agreement among groups for the purpose of living in peace.
2. The Grand Council dealt with matters that affected all the nations in the Confederacy. So each nation's council dealt with matters that affected only their nation.
3. *Matrilineal* comes from words that mean "mother" and "a direct line." The clan people belonged to was passed down from mother to child so it was passed down in a direct line from the mother to the child.
4. The Great Law of Peace provided a way to settle differences by thinking and negotiating rather than violence and warfare. This would stop the nations from fighting with each other so people would not be killed. They could spend more time making their lives better.
5. The Clan Mothers still select chiefs. They still help the chiefs do a good job by providing advice and guidance. Women still own property.
6. The five nations were the Mohawk, Oneida, Onondaga, Cayuga, and Seneca.

First Nations Inventions, pp. 57–59

1. A kayak is narrow and pointed at both ends. This could help it to move through waterways that might be partly blocked by ice. The paddle used with a kayak has a blade on each end. That means a person can paddle a kayak alone and can paddle through narrow passageways. A person using a two-sided paddle can generate speed without moving his or her body much. This is helpful because the person is probably wearing lots of clothes to stay warm, and it is hard to move when you are wearing a lot of layers.
2. Possible answers: dad, mom, Anna, radar, level, solos, sagas, Hannah.
3. You can make syrup by boiling the sap, and you can make maple candy by pouring the boiled syrup into the snow.
4. Getting Around: This paragraph talks about different ways First Nations people get from place to place more quickly. M-m-m-maple Syrup: This paragraph talks about how First Nations people made maple syrup and taught the European explorers how to do the same thing. Those Pesky Bugs: This paragraph talks about the different ways First Nations people used the plants and trees around them to prevent bug bites, treat bug bites, and generally stay healthy. What Else?: This paragraph talks about other inventions by First Nations.
5. Sample answer: I think it is important to be able to get around quickly and easily so that we are not too tired to do the job we need to do when we get to where we need to be. Getting around quickly also means that jobs take less time to do, giving us more time to spend with our friends and families.
6. Sample answer: Vitamin C is a vitamin that is found in many fruits and vegetables. I get my vitamin C by drinking orange juice in the morning before school. I think it was important for First Nations people to find other ways to get vitamin C because they did not have fruits and vegetables in the winter when it snowed and they could not get fruits and vegetables from far away the way we can. People need vitamin C to stay healthy.
7. Answers will vary.

Samuel de Champlain: The Father of New France, pp. 60–61

1. Starting in the 1500s, explorers came to North America and claimed land for their countries. These countries were France, Britain, and Spain. The map shows that in the 1600s, France had most of the land in eastern North America. New France included land from around the Great Lakes all the way down to Louisiana. Britain claimed land along the coast. This was the Thirteen Colonies. They also claimed land above New France and around Hudson's Bay. This was called Rupert's Land. Spain claimed land in the south. There was a lot of land that was not claimed by anyone.
2. The text is organized by time (chronologically). It tells things in the order they happened. This is a good way to organize information about someone's life (biography) because it makes sense to tell things about people from the beginning of their lives to the end.
3. *Accomplishments* mean the things that a person does. The text says that the list tells about Champlain's accomplishments, and in the list are things that he did.
4. *Alliance* and *allies* have the same root word. They come from the same word. Alliance is a thing or idea. Champlain formed an alliance with the Huron and Algonquin. Allies are people. Champlain's allies were the First Nations peoples.
5. Champlain formed an alliance with the Huron and Algonquin. The Iroquois were enemies of the Huron and Algonquin. Champlain fought against the Iroquois to help the Huron and Algonquin. So the Iroquois became the enemies of the French too.
6. Champlain explored and mapped much of New France such as the St. Lawrence River and the Atlantic coast. Champlain founded colonies such as Saint Croix Island, Port Royal, and Quebec City. From 1620 on, he governed New France except for when he was a prisoner in England.

Fur Traders and Settlers in New France, pp. 62–63

1. Fur traders came to get furs. Settlers came to farm. Differences: Fur traders spent most of their time trading for furs with First Nations people. They explored new land looking for furs. Settlers lived in permanent settlements. They spent most of their time growing crops.
2. Sample answer: I learned that the women were all single and some were orphaned. They were chosen because the single women were looking for husbands, and the orphaned women did not have families that would not want them to go. They had to be single so they could get married in New France.
3. Some settlers worked in the fur trade to get more money because they would not make a lot of money from farming. They had to build their farms and pay taxes so they probably did not have a lot of money to buy other things that they needed.
4. The fur traders got their furs from the First Nations people. They traded things with the First Nations people for the furs. The First Nations people hunted to get furs to trade. Some fur traders married First Nations women.

5. Before, they would only hunt for what they needed. Then they started hunting animals for their fur only. Some animals became endangered.

Old Money, New Money, pp. 64–65
1. You might wish to ask a few students to share with the class.
2. People stopped using large stone donuts as money because they were too heavy to use easily.
3. "Put your money where your mouth is" means you stand by what you say.
4. Coins are made of metal, which lasts longer than paper. Coins do not have to be replaced as frequently as bills. This makes coins less expensive to produce and better for the environment.
5. Bills could be made of stronger materials with more detailed patterns on them. Coins could also have complex designs and be made of metals that are difficult to obtain.
6. You might wish to make a display of students' drawings.

The Pony Express, pp. 66–67
1. Sample answer: I think the riders used a relay system because then the riders and horses would have a chance to rest, and people and horses with lots of energy could take over the process.
2. Pony Express riders faced many dangers, including wild animals such as wolves and poisonous snakes, angry Native Americans, rainstorms and snowstorms, burning hot sun, raging rivers they had to cross, bridges that were damaged, injuries to their horses, outlaws, thieves, slippery trails, etc.
3. The telegraph was replaced by the telephone, television, computers, Internet, cell phones, and smart phones, Facebook, Twitter, Google+, blogs, and more.
4. Horses are used today by riders in ceremonies and parades. They also take people where cars and other vehicles cannot go, in search-and-rescue missions or over wilderness areas where vehicles would damage delicate plants and soil or animals. Since horses are quieter than vehicles with motors, they are used in nature reserves. Horses continue to be used for transportation in many countries and to pull carts and wagons. Horse racing is also still popular. Calm horses are used as therapy horses or to help people with disabilities.
5. This text is about moving mail more quickly across the United States. People invented the Pony Express to solve this problem. The first Pony Express ride was on April 3, 1860. It started in San Francisco and headed to St. Louis. The Pony Express used a relay system. The first Pony Express ride proved to be dangerous, but it was also much quicker. The Pony Express only lasted 18 months before it was replaced by the telegraph.

Mount Everest, pp.68–69
1. Students should choose any three of the following dangers: altitude sickness, avalanches, low oxygen levels, blizzards, high winds
2. The first people to make it to the top and back down safely were Edmund Hillary and Tenzing Norgay Sherpa.
3. I think the word *summit* means the top or the highest point. In the second-last paragraph, I read that "people had been trying to get to the top of Everest." In the next sentence, the author tells us about the first people to "reach the summit" and come back down. So the summit must be the top.
4. Sample answer: These names show how important the mountain is to them and how much it affects their lives.
5. Sample answer: Sherpa climbers are known as "Tigers of the Snow" because they live and work in the snowy, high-mountain area and are brave and tough as tigers.
6. Ensure students' organizers show advantages and disadvantages.

The Great Wall of China, pp. 70–71
1. Hang-tu is the process used to create the wall. Frames were created using wood or bamboo. The frames were placed where the wall would stand and dirt was poured into them. The workers would pound the dirt down until it was hard and stable, then move on to a new part of the wall.
2. Answers will vary.
3. A wall would no longer separate or protect a country today due to more powerful modern weaponry, as well as improved communications technologies, including the Internet, smart phones, etc.
4. The main idea of this section is that the Great Wall was built to keep enemies out of China and to protect its culture from other people. Today the Great Wall is a tourist attraction. It no longer blocks other countries from influencing or taking part in Chinese culture.
5. There are graceful arches around the doorways and windows in the Great Wall. The Great Wall itself flows across the land with elegant twists and curves. Detailed carvings decorate the Great Wall and its towers and gates.

William's Windmill, pp. 72–74
1. William's life has changed in these ways: he has written books, he has had a movie made about him, he has spoken at conferences around the world, he has become famous, he has finished high school, and he has gone to a university.
2. This text tells me that because his family was poor and there was a famine in his village, William had to drop out of school at age 14. This text also tells me that despite dropping out of school, William did not put his brain to rest. He did not like that the candles his family used for light made his sister cough, so he started to think of solutions.
3. Villagers may have laughed at William because they did not understand what he was trying to do and did not want to admit it. Perhaps they could not accept that a boy could do something they could not do themselves. They had never seen anything like what William was creating and did not know how to react to it, so they chose to laugh. Also, the windmill probably looked funny since it was built of old bits and pieces.
4. The name Cheetah was chosen because these big cats are strong, powerful, and fast. They have to be clever and creative to hunt down their prey. A cheetah is also an animal that most people in Africa would know.
5. William may have felt happy, relieved, proud, surprised, grateful, satisfied, content, rewarded, pleased, excited, smart, etc.
6. Answers will vary.

What Is in a Symbol? pp. 75–76
1. A symbol can represent an idea or a place. A national symbol represents a country.
2. *Majestic* means something that looks wonderful and powerful. The text says that the bald eagle and the polar bear are majestic. They are both powerful animals. They both look as though they could be the leaders of where they live.
3. The bald eagle is not a good symbol for the United States. The bald eagle has a bad character. He is dishonest. He is lazy. He watches other birds catch fish, then he steals

the fish from them. The turkey is a much better bird. It is respectable and it is a native of America.

4. The beaver is a rodent.
5. The beaver was responsible for the beginning and growth of Canada.
6. David Morrison says that countries get the animals they deserve. When he describes the beaver, he is describing Canadians because Canadians got the animal that they deserved. Canadians believe in the qualities of the beaver.

Morse Code, pp. 77–78

1. a) Morse code is easy to understand.
   b) •• / •–•• •• –•– • / •–• • •– –•• •• –• ––• /
   •– –••• ––– ••– – / –• • •–– / •• –•• • •– ••• /
2. There needed to be an electric wire.
3. Sample answer: I think they would be used at sea. Boats could send messages to people that could see the light but they would not need any machine to hear the message.
4. *Destination* means the place where you want something to end up. The text says that messages were sent across wires to their destination, so destination must mean the place the messages were going to.
5. Sample answer: It means that someone is in danger and needs to be saved before they die.
6. This text is fact. I know this because everything in it is true. You can check to find out if what is in the text is true by looking in books or on the Internet. Everyone would agree that the text is true.

Penicillin Saves the World, pp. 79–80

1. Sample answer: When Fleming first saw how the mold had destroyed the bacteria, he may have felt amazed, curious, surprised, fascinated, interested, puzzled, etc.
2. Answers will vary.
3. Sample answer: Doctors were probably very glad they could finally help more people.
4. Answers will vary.
5. Sample answer: Because it happened a long time ago, people know about a discovery but not who discovered it.
6. This quote means that scientists must constantly be open to new ideas and that they should examine their experiment results carefully. They should not have such a strong idea of how their experiment will turn out that they do not notice even small variations.

How Compasses Changed the World, pp. 81–83

1. Sample answer: I think the name *compass* was chosen because compasses measure where the user is in relation to the magnetic North Pole.
2. Ensure students write 3 sentences.
3. Sample answer: Einstein's quote means that inventors and experimenters cannot expect everything to always happen as they expect. They should have the courage to try anyway and to be smart enough to learn from their mistakes.
4. Sample answer: When people explored the world, they came into contact with other cultures. They heard new languages, ate new foods, saw new ways of doing things. They took some of these new ideas and goods home and probably shared some of their experiences with the new people they met. Sometimes the cultures got along and sometimes the result was war.
5. Answers will vary. Ensure that students explain their thinking.

Comets, pp. 84–87

1. a) They are all space rocks. They are left over from the formation of the solar system. They orbit the Sun.
   b) A comet is made of dust and ice. Comets are from 1 to 10 kilometres across but can be up to 100 kilometres. Some comets pass close to the Sun. They have a tail when they pass by the Sun. Then we can see them.
   c) Asteroids are made from rocks and metals. They range in size from less than one kilometre across to hundreds of kilometres across.
   d) Meteoroids are small and rocky. They are formed from the dust of a comet or pieces of an asteroid. They can be tiny like a piece of dust or up to 10 metres across. Sometimes they fall to Earth and burn in the atmosphere. Some do not burn up completely and land on Earth.
2. Students' organizers should show the differences in size and composition of the 4 types of space rocks.
3. Same: Comets come from both these places.
   Different: The Kuiper Belt is a flat disk that begins beyond Neptune. The Oort Cloud is round like a ball and surrounds the whole solar system. Short-period comets come from the Kuiper Belt. Long-period comets from the Oort Cloud.
4. Halley's comet came from the Kuiper Belt. Hale-Bopp came from the Oort Cloud.
5. All the subheadings are questions. They help me because I know that the information after each subheading will help me answer the question.
6. Some of the information may not be true because the author says that scientists think that things happen one way but they are not sure.
7. Answers will vary.

It Came From Space, pp. 88–89

1. Space exploration only started in 1957. People have been on Earth for thousands of years.
2. It might be important if someone needed blood right away and the doctor had to find out what kind of blood the person needed. It could save time if a doctor wanted to check the blood of a person before saying what was wrong with the person.
3. Sample answer: I think it means something that is made from something that was done before. This is a good word for the technologies because they all came from ideas or things first made for space exploration.
4. Sample answer: It is a satellite that goes around Earth but it is made by people.
5. The central idea is that many products we use today came from technology developed for space exploration. The author supports this idea by giving examples of things we use today that were first made for space exploration.
6. The author thinks these technologies are great things. The author calls them amazing, and says that they make our lives better.

Scientific Classification, pp. 90–91

1. Organisms in these kingdoms are usually so tiny that we cannot see them without a microscope. So most people probably have not seen any.
2. A domestic cat belongs to the animal kingdom, the chordate phylum, the mammal class, and the carnivore order.
3. Sample answer: They come from the genus and species name of the cat. The first name is the genus name and the last name is the species name. I have two names too but I have a first name and a last or family name. Together my two names tell who I am, just like the names of organisms tell what they are.

4. Sample answer: Scientists need to be able to understand each other so they can share what they learn. If scientists in different parts of the world used a different classification system or naming system, it would be hard for them to understand which organisms they were talking about.
5. Sample answer: A triangle with one pointed end at the bottom would work best. There is less and less space in the triangle (a smaller area) as you move down from the top to the bottom. This is like the number of organisms in each category—there are fewer and fewer as you move from kingdom to species.
6. The third paragraph explains that there are seven categories and gives the names of the categories. The list describes each category using a cat as an example.

Symbiosis, pp. 92–93
1. It is not symbiosis because the relationship between the animals must be one that goes on for a long period of time. Eating another animal is something that is quick, then it is done.
2. Symbiosis is a long-term relationship between two different species. Mutualism, commensalism, and parasitism are three kinds of symbiosis. In mutualism, both species gain something from the relationship. Neither species is hurt. In commensalism, one species benefits from the relationship while the other species is not harmed. In parasitism, one organism lives on or in another organism and gets its nourishment from the other organism. The other organism is harmed in some way
3. Mutualism is introduced by explaining the root word *mutual*, then giving the definition. Commensalism is introduced by giving the definition of the word only.
4. Sample answer: The cattle do not really deliver the food to the egrets, but they do make it easier for the egrets to find insects. So the word is used in a way that is different from its real meaning. The quotation marks show the reader this.
5. Sample answer: The author is giving the definition as it is used in biology. This makes me think that the word has more than one meaning.
6. Sample answer: The title tells that the whole text is about symbiosis. The subheadings are three different kinds of symbiosis. This helps me because I know that the text under each subheading will be about one idea. It also helps me remember that mutualism, commensalism, and parasitism are all types of symbiosis.

Working Together, pp. 94–95
1. The two types of adaptations are physical and behavioural. Physical adaptations are structures on or in the animal. One example is beaks. Behavioural adaptations are things animals do. One example is hibernation.
2. It is a behavioural adaptation.
3. Sample answer: The fungus cannot live outside the ant's colony and it cannot reproduce without the help of the ants.
4. The sentence is "Common examples of group cooperation are insects that live in colonies, such as bees and ants." *Familiar* is the closest in meaning.
5. The main idea is that some animals live in cooperative groups to survive. The main idea is introduced in the second paragraph. The author develops the main idea by describing examples of cooperative groups. These groups are leaf-cutter ants and meerkats.
6. Sample answer: The first paragraph is about survival in animals. It explains what animals need to do to survive and explains about two types of characteristics of animals that help them survive. I think the author wanted to review what survival was before explaining about one way animals survive. The author wanted to make sure that the reader would understand what the text was about.

Autumn Days, pp. 96–97
1. Chlorophyll makes leaves green. In autumn, leaves stop making food and the chlorophyll disappears. The yellows and oranges that are hidden in the leaves are now visible. Some leaves are red because they contain a sugar called glucose.
2. Deciduous trees lose their leaves in the fall. Students should list two of the following examples: maples, oaks, and birches. Coniferous trees stay green all winter and do not lose their leaves. Students should list two of the following examples: pines, spruces, and firs.
3. The ptarmigan prepares for winter by changing colour. The bird replaces its brown feathers with off-white feathers. The white feathers make the ptarmigan difficult to see against the winter snow.
4. Answers might vary, but most students will say they notice the air is colder, the days are shorter (it gets dark earlier), and the leaves change colour and fall off the trees.
5. Hibernating animals begin to eat a lot in the autumn because they need to put on lots of fat to give them the energy they will need while they are sleeping through the winter.
6. Answers might vary. Sample answer: These animals hibernate because the foods they eat are very hard to find during the winter. Students may also suggest that some animals cannot handle the cold weather so they stay warm below the ground or in caves.

Stick It, pp. 98–99
1. A negatively charged object has more electrons than protons. A positively charged object has more protons than electrons.
2. If you rubbed the balloon for a long time, more electrons would move to it from the wool. This would make a stronger negative charge on the balloon because it would have more electrons. It should stick to the wall longer.
3. Sample answer: *Neutron* is very close to *neutral*. A neutron has no charge, so it makes sense that its name is close to neutral.
4. To understand what static electricity is, you have to understand what electrons and protons are. To understand electrons and protons, you need to know about atoms.
5. Sample answer: Drawing the diagram helped me because I had to read the information again and that made me think more about it. I will probably remember what happens better because I drew the diagram.

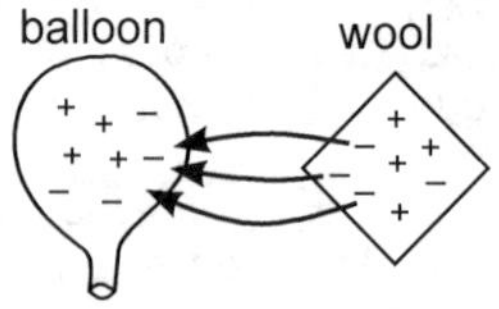

6. Sample answer: The diagram and text give about the same information. The diagram makes it clearer that the protons and neutrons are bunched together to make the nucleus, and the electrons are around the nucleus. Sometimes it helps to see a diagram or picture of something you have read. It helps you understand better.